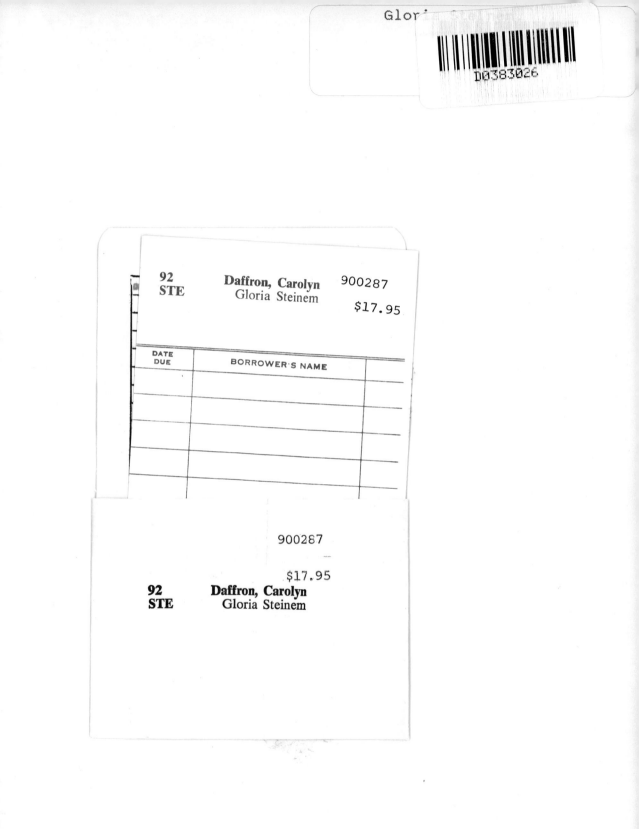

**92
STE** **Daffron, Carolyn**   900287
Gloria Steinem

$17.95

DATE DUE	BORROWER'S NAME	

900287

$17.95

**92
STE** **Daffron, Carolyn**
Gloria Steinem

GLORIA STEINEM

AMERICAN WOMEN of ACHIEVEMENT

GLORIA STEINEM

CAROLYN DAFFRON

CHELSEA HOUSE PUBLISHERS

NEW YORK   PHILADELPHIA

EDITOR-IN-CHIEF: Nancy Toff
EXECUTIVE EDITOR: Remmel T. Nunn
MANAGING EDITOR: Karyn Gullen Browne
COPY CHIEF: Juliann Barbato
PICTURE EDITOR: Adrian G. Allen
ART DIRECTOR: Giannella Garrett
MANUFACTURING MANAGER: Gerald Levine

Staff for GLORIA STEINEM:

SENIOR EDITOR: Elisa Petrini
ASSISTANT EDITOR: Maria Behan
EDITORIAL ASSISTANT: Karen Schimmel
COPYEDITOR: Ellen Scordato
PICTURE RESEARCH: Karen Herman
DESIGNER: Design Oasis
PRODUCTION COORDINATOR: Laura McCormick
COVER ILLUSTRATION: John Schreck

CREATIVE DIRECTOR: Harold Steinberg

3 5 7 9 8 6 4

Library of Congress Cataloging in Publication Data

Daffron, Carolyn. GLORIA STEINEM

(American women of achievement)
Bibliography: p.
Includes index.
1. Steinem, Gloria—Juvenile literature. 2. Feminists—United
States—Biography—Juvenile literature. [1. Steinem, Gloria.
2. Feminists] I. Title. II. Series.
HQ1413.S675D34   1987   305.4′2′0924 [B] [92]   87-6640

ISBN 1-55546-679-6
     0-7910-0422-8 (pbk.)

CONTENTS

"Remember the Ladies"—Matina S. Horner 7

1. "I Have Sisters" 13

2. Daughter of Two Children 23

3. The Education of an Activist Writer 37

4. Starting Out 47

5. A Double Life 57

6. Feminist Awakening 67

7. Gains and Setbacks 79

8. Milestones 93

Further Reading 106

Chronology 107

Index 108

AMERICAN WOMEN of ACHIEVEMENT

Abigail Adams
women's rights advocate

Jane Addams
social worker

Louisa May Alcott
author

Marian Anderson
singer

Susan B. Anthony
woman suffragist

Ethel Barrymore
actress

Clara Barton
founder of the American Red Cross

Elizabeth Blackwell
physician

Nellie Bly
journalist

Margaret Bourke-White
photographer

Pearl Buck
author

Rachel Carson
biologist and author

Mary Cassatt
artist

Agnes De Mille
choreographer

Emily Dickinson
poet

Isadora Duncan
dancer

Amelia Earhart
aviator

Mary Baker Eddy
founder of the Christian Science church

Betty Friedan
feminist

Althea Gibson
tennis champion

Emma Goldman
political activist

Helen Hayes
actress

Lillian Hellman
playwright

Katharine Hepburn
actress

Karen Horney
psychoanalyst

Anne Hutchinson
religious leader

Mahalia Jackson
gospel singer

Helen Keller
humanitarian

Jeane Kirkpatrick
diplomat

Emma Lazarus
poet

Clare Boothe Luce
author and diplomat

Barbara McClintock
biologist

Margaret Mead
anthropologist

Edna St. Vincent Millay
poet

Julia Morgan
architect

Grandma Moses
painter

Louise Nevelson
sculptor

Sandra Day O'Connor
Supreme Court justice

Georgia O'Keeffe
painter

Eleanor Roosevelt
diplomat and humanitarian

Wilma Rudolph
champion athlete

Florence Sabin
medical researcher

Beverly Sills
opera singer

Gertrude Stein
author

Gloria Steinem
feminist

Harriet Beecher Stowe
author and abolitionist

Mae West
entertainer

Edith Wharton
author

Phillis Wheatley
poet

Babe Didrikson Zaharias
champion athlete

CHELSEA HOUSE PUBLISHERS

"Remember the Ladies"

MATINA S. HORNER

Remember the Ladies." That is what Abigail Adams wrote to her husband John, then a delegate to the Continental Congress, as the Founding Fathers met in Philadelphia to form a new nation in March of 1776. "Be more generous and favorable to them than your ancestors. Do not put such unlimited power in the hands of the Husbands. If particular care and attention is not paid to the Ladies," Abigail Adams warned, "we are determined to foment a Rebellion, and will not hold ourselves bound by any Laws in which we have no voice, or Representation."

The words of Abigail Adams, one of the earliest American advocates of women's rights, were prophetic. Because when we have not "remembered the ladies," they have, by their words and deeds, reminded us so forcefully of the omission that we cannot fail to remember them. For the history of American women is as interesting and varied as the history of our nation as a whole. American women have played an integral part in founding, settling, and building our country. Some we remember as remarkable women who—against great odds—achieved distinction in the public arena: Anne Hutchinson, who in the 17th century became a charismatic religious leader; Phillis Wheatley, an 18th-century black slave who became a poet; Susan B. Anthony, whose name is synonymous with the 19th-century women's rights movement, and who led the struggle to enfranchise women; and, in our own century, Amelia Earhart, the first woman to cross the Atlantic Ocean by air.

These extraordinary women certainly merit our admiration, but other women, "common women," many of them all but forgotten, should also be recognized for their contributions to American thought and culture. Women have been community builders; they have founded schools and formed voluntary associations to help those in need; they have assumed the major responsibility for rearing children, passing on from one generation to the next the values that keep a culture alive. These and innumerable other contributions, once ignored, are now being recognized by scholars, students, and the public. It is exciting and gratifying to realize that a part of our history that was hardly acknowledged a few generations ago is now being studied and brought to light.

In recent decades, the field of women's history has grown from obscurity to a politically controversial splinter movement to academic respectability, in many cases mainstreamed into such traditional disciplines as history, economics, and psychology. Scholars of women, both female and male, have organized research centers at such prestigious institutions as Wellesley College, Stanford University, and the University of California. Other notable centers for women's studies are the Center for the American Woman and Politics at the Eagleton Institute of Politics at Rutgers University, the Henry A. Murray Research Center for the Study of Lives, at Radcliffe College, and the Women's Research and Education Institute, the research arm of the Congressional Caucus on Women's Issues. Other scholars and public figures have established archives and libraries, such as the Schlesinger Library on the History of Women in America, at Radcliffe College, and the Sophia Smith Collection, at Smith College, to collect and preserve the written and tangible legacies of women.

From the initial donation of the Women's Rights Collection in 1943, the Schlesinger Library grew to encompass vast collections documenting the manifold accomplishments of American women. Simultaneously, the women's movement in general and the academic discipline of women's studies in particular also began with a narrow definition and gradually expanded their mandate. Early causes such as woman suffrage and social reform, abolition and organized labor were joined by newer concerns such as the history of women in business and the professions and in politics and government; the study of the family; and social issues such as health policy and education.

Women, as historian Arthur M. Schlesinger, jr., once pointed out, "have constituted the most spectacular casualty of traditional history. They have made up at least half the human race, but you could never tell that by looking at the books historians write." The new breed of historians is remedying that omission. They have written books about immigrant women and about working-class women who struggled for survival in cities and about black women who met the challenges of life in rural areas. They are telling the stories of women who, despite the barriers of tradition and economics, became lawyers and doctors and public figures.

The women's studies movement has also led scholars to question traditional interpretations of their respective disciplines. For example, the study of war has traditionally been an exercise in military and political analysis, an examination of strategies planned and executed by men. But scholars of women's history have pointed out that wars have also been periods of tremendous change and even opportunity for women, because the very absence of men on the home front enabled them to expand their educational, economic, and professional activities and to assume leadership in their homes.

The early scholars of women's history showed a unique brand of courage in choosing to investigate new subjects and take new approaches to old ones. Often, like their subjects, they endured criticism and even ostracism by their academic colleagues. But their efforts have unquestionably been worthwhile, because with the publication of each new study and book another piece of the historical patchwork is sewn into place, revealing an increasingly comprehensive picture of the role of women in our rich and varied history.

Such books on groups of women are essential, but books that focus on the lives of individuals are equally indispensable. Biographies can be inspirational, offering their readers the example of people with vision who have looked outside themselves for their goals and have often struggled against great obstacles to achieve them. Marian Anderson, for instance, had to overcome racial bigotry in order to perfect her art and perform as a concert singer. Isadora Duncan defied the rules of classical dance to find true artistic freedom. Jane Addams had to break down society's notions of the proper role for women in order to create new social institutions, notably the settlement house. All of these women had to come to terms both with themselves and with the world in which they lived. Only then could they move ahead as pioneers in their chosen callings.

Biography can inspire not only by adulation but also by realism. It helps us to see not only the qualities in others that we hope to emulate, but also, perhaps, the weaknesses that made them "human." By helping us identify with the subject on a more personal level they help us to feel that we, too, can achieve such goals. We read about Eleanor Roosevelt, for instance, who occupied a unique and seemingly enviable position as the wife of the president. Yet we can sympathize with her inner dilemma: an inherently shy woman, she had to force herself to live a most public life in order to use her position to benefit others. We may not be able to imagine ourselves having the immense poetic talent of Emily Dickinson, but from her story we can understand the challenges faced by a creative woman who was expected to fulfill many family responsibilities. And though few of us will ever reach the level of athletic accomplishment displayed by Wilma Rudolph or Babe Zaharias, we can still appreciate their spirit, their overwhelming will to excel.

A biography is a multifaceted lens. It is first of all a magnification, the intimate examination of one particular life. But at the same time, it is a wide-angle lens, informing us about the world in which the subject lived. We come away from reading about one life knowing more about the social, political, and economic fabric of the time. It is for this reason, perhaps, that the great New England essayist Ralph Waldo Emerson wrote, in 1841, "There is properly no history: only biography." And it is also why biography, and particularly women's biography, will continue to fascinate writers and readers alike.

GLORIA STEINEM

World renowned as a symbol of the women's liberation movement, Gloria Steinem has discovered that fame can pose special problems: The public is sometimes more interested in her as a celebrity than as a spokeswoman for the causes she endorses.

ONE

"I Have Sisters"

In 1971 Gloria Steinem was a media superstar. Anyone who read *Time*, *Newsweek*, or watched television talk shows could recognize her attractive, intelligent face framed by her trademark blue-tinted aviator glasses and mane of gold-streaked hair. Her wit and charm were legendary. She was famous all over America as the leader of the new movement—or, as some saw it, the passing fad—called feminism or women's liberation, that sought to end discrimination against women and to allow women the opportunity to go beyond their traditional roles.

Steinem was delighted that women's liberation had become a major social issue. She had worked tirelessly to publicize the movement, writing and lecturing every day and often sleeping only four hours a night.

But she was not always pleased by all the attention devoted to her personally, which was sometimes hostile, even insulting. During one television interview an actor got so angry at her that he snarled, "If you weren't a woman, I'd hit you right in the mouth." (Steinem had the last word. Without missing a beat, she replied, "Go ahead! At least you'd be taking a woman seriously for once.") An article in *Esquire* later that year called her "the intellectual's pinup" and hinted that she owed her success to her shapely legs and her string of powerful boyfriends, not to her talent or the importance of her ideas.

The *Esquire* article upset her for weeks, but in some ways, the "favorable" stories and interviews were even worse. For one thing, it bothered her when the press acted as if she had somehow been elected leader of all dissatisfied women. Steinem did not presume to speak for all women, or even for all feminists. And it angered her when, instead of debating her ideas, the media reported admiringly on her appearance and her stylish wardrobe, or the glamorous life she led during the

1960s as one of New York's "beautiful people."

At 36, Steinem was a skillful writer with passionate beliefs and more than 15 years' experience, yet more articles were printed *about* her than *by* her. True, she was a staff commentator for fashionable *New York* magazine and could also have gotten dozens of free-lance assignments—but not on women's rights issues. "We've done our feminist article already," the big magazines would tell her. No one in the mainstream press seemed to take the women's movement seriously, or to think that Americans wanted to read about it.

Steinem finally decided that the only way to ensure a market for ideas such as hers was for feminists to start their own national magazine. A few phone calls convinced her that many other women writers and activists agreed. She invited some of them to the first of several meetings in her Manhattan apartment, and the idea of *Ms.* magazine was born.

First-time visitors to Steinem's apartment on the second floor of an old East Side brownstone must have been surprised at how simply she lived. The apartment had two rooms. The front room was decorated in the bright oranges, pinks, yellows, and purples popular in the 1960s. It had an elevated sleeping loft above an alcove filled with oversized Oriental pillows and knick-knacks from the two years she had lived in India. The back room, her office, held a battered desk and a rocker. On the wall Steinem had tacked posters of her heroes: politician Bobby Kennedy; her friend César Chávez, who was organizing California's farmworkers; writer Karen Blixen, who had published under the name of Isak Dinesen; and Jeanne Moreau, Steinem's favorite actress. Newspapers and magazines littered the floor.

The women settled in among the bright cushions and began to consider the hard, exciting task ahead of them. They agreed that the magazine should be owned by women. It should report truthfully about job discrimination, changing sex roles, and the need for women to work together—*not* about such traditional women's-magazine subjects as cooking, fashion, housekeeping, and strategies to attract men. The proposed publication should let women know where they could turn for help and support. It should be a commercial magazine available on newsstands all over the country, not just another of the many mail-order feminist newsletters and small local publications that had appeared over the past few years. Ideally, the magazine should make a profit that could be used to support other feminist projects. The needs and goals were clear. But where would they find the money to get started?

Steinem relaxes in the New York apartment where Ms. *magazine was planned. An early 1970s caption for this photo noted that "Gloria Steinem, writer-activist-antiwar gorgeous bachelor girl, has managed to make the whole world accessible to her."*

Over the months that followed, Steinem and her colleagues developed hundreds of article ideas for the new magazine. They did mock-ups of designs and sample illustrations and drafted a proposed budget. They even decided on the magazine's name: *Ms.*, the form of address most feminists preferred to "Mrs." or "Miss," because like

"Mr." it allowed women to be identified as individuals, not by marital status. Armed with these detailed plans, the women tried to find financial backing. For months they called every investor they could think of, made appointments, and were turned down flat again and again.

When she asked potential investors

Steinem's friend and fellow activist, United Farm Workers president César Chávez (center), leads a San Francisco protest against nonunion employers in 1979.

their reasons for refusing to back *Ms.*, Steinem was told that the venture was just too risky: Established magazines were failing every month. Besides, the *Ms.* founders wanted to keep a 51 percent interest in the magazine, to ensure that contributors could express their ideas without outside interference. The investment experts also took issue with the *Ms.* founders' charitable goals—who ever heard of a magazine that wanted to give its profits to social causes? Investors were out to make money, not to support a bunch of inexperienced "Women's Libbers."

As months passed, Steinem and her colleagues began to think they would have to change their idea of *Ms.*, or give up the project completely. But feminists around the country assured them that there was a huge audience who needed *Ms.* and who would buy it. More and more women heard about the proposed magazine and volunteered their time, talent, and business advice. Then Katharine Graham of the *Washington Post*, the only woman among the nation's top newspaper publishers, contributed some hard cash—enough to cover expenses for a few months.

Soon afterward Clay Felker, Steinem's editor and publisher at *New York* magazine and a longtime friend, made a highly unusual offer. He agreed to include a shortened, sample issue of *Ms.* as an insert to the year-end issue of *New York*. *New York* would also pay for and help produce the first full issue of *Ms.*, called the "Preview Issue." In return *Ms.* would give *New York* all its advertising revenues and part of the profits (if any) from sales of the Preview Issue. And the sample issue of *Ms.* would give *New York* a splashy, provocative year-end issue, one that was sure to start people talking.

The *Ms.* founders joyfully accepted Felker's offer. *New York*'s wide readership would guarantee that the short insert would be read by thousands in the New York area. And the full Preview Issue was just the nationwide test *Ms.* needed to see how many people across America would purchase a feminist magazine.

With Steinem as a founding editor, *Ms.* set up shop in September 1971. Its tiny office was cramped and ill-equipped, with no copier, no water cooler, and not enough desks to go around. Its core of four editors—Letty Cottin Pogrebin, a well-known author and publicist; Joanne Edgar, a journalist and political activist; Mary Peacock, editor of an underground fashion magazine, *Rags*; and Nina Finkelstein, a book editor—were its only full-time employees (all unpaid) and were aided by as many part-time volunteers as they could find. Everyone worked at a frantic pace. It seemed that a new emergency arose every day: Authors canceled out at the last minute, articles

Steinem (center) meets with Patricia Carbine (left), who became the publisher of Ms., *and publisher Katharine Graham, who provided funding for the fledgling magazine.*

were left unfinished, and they had barely two months to prepare both the Preview Issue and the *New York* magazine insert.

Nevertheless, as the members of the *Ms.* staff later reported, "The work got done and the decisions got made. They happened communally. . . we just chose not to do anything with which one of us strongly disagreed." It might have been chaotic, but by early December, journalist Pamela Howard recounted, the *Ms.* office radiated "the same kind of electricity that crackles in the air at the opening of a play." Steinem's own excitement was mixed with dread. What if all those financial experts were right after all? She was doubly anxious when she thought about how she, *Ms.*, and the feminist movement were so closely identified in the press. If *Ms.* succeeded where other

Feminists picket the Miss America Pageant, charging that the contest sets false goals for women. Ms. was targeted both at readers already committed to women's liberation and at people who were just curious about the idea.

new magazines had failed, it would be due in part to her personal reputation. And if *Ms.* bombed and made feminism look foolish, would that be her fault, too? Steinem had many detractors in 1971—not just opponents of women's liberation, but also some feminists who thought she was trying to create a slick magazine to advance her own career.

On December 20, when the year-end issue of *New York* hit the stands, *Ms.* staffers held their breath. But by the end of the month, it set a newsstand record—the ground-breaking insert sold more copies of *New York* than ever before in the magazine's history. More importantly, however, it proved that there was a vast new audience of readers, women waiting for a magazine that addressed their changing world.

Steinem was elated, but still worried about the future: How would the full-

The predominantly female staff of Ms. *assembles for a group portrait in the early 1970s. "Trying to start a magazine controlled by its female staff in a world accustomed to the authority of men," Steinem once wryly observed, "should be the subject of a musical comedy."*

length Preview Issue fare outside sophisticated New York City? The *Ms.* staff had decided to print 300,000 copies—a huge number for a new venture—in the hope that it would stay on the stands for several months and establish a strong image. But if the magazine failed, the enormous print run would make it a very expensive gamble.

The Preview Issue was finished on time, but just barely. It included articles on housewives who are treated as "household appendages" instead of individuals and women who are conditioned to fear success. There was a how-to piece on writing a marriage contract and a feminist rating of the 1972 presidential candidates. The lead article, written by Steinem, was called

"Sisterhood." In it she described how, in just a few years, she had changed from a "girl reporter"—proud to work among men and be thought *almost* their equal—to a committed feminist spokeswoman.

The Preview Issue was distributed across America in January 1972. To help publicize it, *Ms.* staffers and writers launched a nationwide tour, explaining their goals to women's groups and on any radio or television shows that would have them. But when Steinem and the others reached their first few stops, there were no copies of *Ms.* to be found. Amazingly—in just a little over a week—the entire first edition had sold out.

The success silenced skeptics once and for all. Not only did the Preview Issue make a handsome profit, but subscriptions were streaming in. Steinem knew that *Ms.* could attract enough investors to survive, at least for a while. But what pleased and touched her most were the letters, thousands a week, that poured in from readers. Women wrote to Steinem and the *Ms.* staff as if they were personal friends. Some letters were funny, some angry, some tragic—but almost all the letter-writers expressed joy at learning that they were not alone, that other women shared their feelings.

Steinem had experienced all the same emotions as her involvement with feminism grew. As she wrote in

Gloria Steinem at the Ms. *office in 1972. The founders of the magazine felt they were providing a needed alternative to traditional women's publications, but even they were surprised by its popularity.*

"Sisterhood," her article for the first issue of *Ms.*:

> I am continually moved to discover I have sisters.
> I am beginning, just beginning, to find out who I am.

When they were first married, Leo and Ruth Steinem looked forward to a bright future together. A decade later, the family was beset by financial and personal misfortune.

TWO

Daughter of Two Children

According to Steinem, her mother, Ruth Nuneviller Steinem, was the daughter of "a handsome railroad-engineer and a schoolteacher who felt she had married 'beneath her.'" Ruth's mother had great ambitions for her daughter, and she scrimped so Ruth could attend Oberlin College, a prestigious school and the first in America to admit blacks and women along with white male students. Ruth was an enthusiastic, talented scholar, but the money soon ran out and she had to move back home. She finished her education by working her way through Toledo State University. There she met and fell in love with Leo Steinem, the charming and witty editor of the university newspaper. Impressed by Ruth's intelligence, creative energy, and sense of humor, Leo invited her to become the paper's literary editor. Soon afterward, they were secretly married.

Leo Steinem came from a prominent family in Toledo. His father, Joseph Steinem, was a successful businessman (although, along with countless others, he would soon lose all his money in the stock market crash of 1929). Pauline Steinem, Leo's mother, was a pioneer in the women's suffrage movement, which fought for, and eventually won, women's right to vote. She was active in many charities, helped write Ohio's first Juvenile Court Law, founded a vocational high school, and was the first woman member of the Toledo Board of Education.

Despite his impressive family background, Leo Steinem was not the man Mrs. Nuneviller would have chosen for her daughter. He was a terrible student, more interested in planning all the school dances than in getting a degree or in finding a steady job. Furthermore, some members of both the Steinem and Nuneviller families objected to "mixed marriages"—the Steinems were Jewish and the Nune-

Steinem's maternal grandmother, Mary Catherine Nuneviller, circa 1886. Many of Ruth Nuneviller's relatives disapproved of her relationship with Leo Steinem because he was "unacceptably Jewish."

reer for the next several years, eventually becoming Sunday editor of one of Toledo's two major dailies. But Gloria, born on March 25, 1934, was never to know this talented, feisty professional. By the time Gloria was born, Ruth Steinem had left the work she loved; been hospitalized for a nervous breakdown; and fallen prey to bouts of depression, delusion, and fear.

Like millions of other Americans, the young Steinem family was hit hard by the Great Depression of the 1930s. During the years before Gloria's birth, Ruth Steinem learned to make soup from leftovers and cut winter clothes from old blankets. But even when times got better, Leo Steinem never could save money or hold down a nine-to-five job. Although he was as well-meaning and charming as ever, he had no sense of financial responsibility. His head was filled with dreams of making it big in show business. One of his least impractical schemes was to try to turn Michigan's isolated Clark Lake into a fancy summer resort that he hoped would attract the "big bands" that were so popular in the 1930s and 1940s. Until Gloria was about 10, she and her family spent their summers at the lake.

During the off-season the Steinems lived a gypsy life, traveling around the country in a trailer while Mr. Steinem tried to make a living buying and selling antiques. They would head for warm climates—Florida one year, Cal-

villers Christian. When Ruth and Leo had a second, public wedding a year after their secret marriage, several relatives from both families refused to attend.

During the early years of married life Ruth Steinem earned a teaching certificate, taught college calculus, and became a much-respected newspaperwoman. Her first daughter, Susanne, was born in 1925. Mrs. Steinem juggled motherhood and her newspaper ca-

A relief worker distributes soup and bread to the unemployed during the Great Depression of the 1930s. Along with millions of Americans, the Steinems suffered financial hardship during this period.

ifornia the next. The family never stayed put long enough for Gloria to attend any school for more than a few weeks at a time. Most of her education came from her mother, who used her teaching certificate to keep suspicious truant officers at bay.

Mrs. Steinem did her best to feed, clothe, and educate her daughters, but as the years went on she slipped deeper into fear and despair. Some-times the old, fun-loving Ruth Steinem would emerge, and she and her daughters would sing and dance together. Mrs. Steinem also taught her daughters a love of books, learning, and poetry. Gloria's early childhood was odd and precarious, but not always unhappy.

Gloria adored her father, whom she remembers as "a sentimental, kind, childish man." Mr. Steinem would take Gloria out for malteds or to the movies,

Steinem spent many childhood summers at this resort in Clark Lake. Fascinated by show business, Leo Steinem hoped to turn the isolated Michigan town into a showplace for the era's "big bands."

where they would watch newsreels about current events or the escapist films popular during the depression and World War II. Gloria also loved helping her father with his antique selling. Long after she was grown she remembered how she would "wrap and unwrap the newspaper around the china and small objects he had bought at auctions and was selling to dealers. It made me feel necessary and grown-up." But interspersed with her father's buying trips were many visits to the finance company, seeking yet another loan to tide the family over until the big break he always anticipated came.

Susanne went away to college when Gloria was eight. Two years later, World War II and gasoline rationing put an end to Leo Steinem's resort. By this time Ruth Steinem was living in a nightmare world of terror and depression and needed constant attention. For years Mr. Steinem had tried to run the house, bring home the groceries, and reassure his wife when she gave way to uncontrollable sadness or imaginary fears. He had tried to be patient, but he was a weak man. When the Clark Lake resort failed, he could no longer tolerate the situation at home. Telling Gloria that he had to travel full-time now to keep his antique business going, Leo Steinem left his family for good.

For the next seven years, Gloria and Ruth Steinem lived alone together, most of the time in Toledo. First they had a basement apartment—a small place, but in a pleasant neighborhood. After they moved in, Gloria "made one last stab at being a child," as she later described it, "by pretending to be much sicker with a cold than I really was." She hoped that this exaggerated illness would transform Mrs. Steinem into a sane, traditional mother who would fuss over her daughter and bring her chicken soup. Gloria's plan failed; Ruth Steinem was too sick to help and only became more depressed that she could not care for the daughter she loved. At the age of 10, Gloria realized that she would have to take charge; she would have to be the parent.

Sometimes Ruth Steinem would lie in bed with her eyes closed all day long, hearing imaginary voices. Other times she would go for days and weeks without sleeping, worried that her loved ones were in danger. There were days when she forgot that World War II had ended, and she was convinced that there were German soldiers outside the house. To escape from her fears and insomnia, Mrs. Steinem became addicted to something she called "Doc Howard's medicine," which Glo-

Five-year-old Gloria Steinem (left) attends a New Orleans Mardi Gras celebration with a young friend.

ria later learned was the strong sedative used to make "Mickey Finns" or "knockout drops." This "medicine" made Mrs. Steinem clumsy and slurred her speech, so that neighbors and Gloria's school friends thought she was drunk. But the alternative was often even worse. One Thanksgiving weekend Mrs. Steinem went without her "medicine" and plunged her hand through a window, cutting it badly. For

Gloria and her older sister Susanne poke their heads out from the family trailer. Until Gloria was 10, the Steinem family lived and traveled in this trailer during the winter.

most of that weekend Gloria hung onto her mother desperately with one hand, while holding *A Tale of Two Cities*, her eighth-grade assignment, in the other.

After the basement apartment, Gloria and Ruth Steinem lived in the upstairs of a yellow farmhouse Mrs. Steinem had inherited from her family. They would remain there for several years. The house, like the East Toledo neighborhood, had seen better days. Its front

porch was sagging, and a noisy state highway ran within a few feet of the windows. In Gloria's grandparents' time, the house had been on the outskirts of town; now a crowded, poor neighborhood had grown up around it. The Steinems and their new neighbors had little in common. "East Toledo," Gloria Steinem recalled years later, was "the kind of place where they beat up the first available black on Saturday night. They considered us nuts on two counts: we read books and we were poorer than they were."

Gloria and her mother lived on the small income they got from leasing Mrs. Steinem's share of the Michigan land where the failed resort had been. For a while they could also rent out the bottom floor of their house, until the health department condemned their furnace as unsafe. From then on they lived without tenants—and without heat. During the winter Gloria and her mother often shared a bed at night for warmth.

Because she now had a permanent home of sorts, Gloria began attending school more regularly. Although she was very intelligent and read a great deal, she could not be a diligent student while running the Steinems' strange household at the same time. On her better days Mrs. Steinem tried to cook and clean, but she rarely got very far. Usually it was Gloria who prepared the meals. For breakfast or supper she would bring her mother "an endless stream of toast and coffee, bologna sandwiches and dime pies, in a child's version of what meals should be." For several years she also worked after school, although she lived in fear that Mrs. Steinem would once again forget where her daughter had gone and call the police. It was humiliating to come home from work on dark winter evenings and find policemen

Olympic figure-skating champion Sonja Henie starred in a number of the escapist movies that were popular during the Great Depression. Leo Steinem took Gloria to see many such films during her youth.

parked in front of the house, with friends and neighbors staring.

In her striking memoir, "Ruth's Song (Because She Could Not Sing It)," Gloria Steinem describes these years with her mother. She remembers "hanging paper drapes I bought in the dime store; stacking books and papers in the shape of two armchairs and covering them with blankets; evolving my own dishwashing system (I waited until all the dishes were dirty, then put them in the bathtub); and listening to my mother's high praise for these housekeeping ef-

Ruth and Gloria Steinem lived in Toledo, Ohio, seen here from an aerial perspective, for seven years. Although times were hard, Steinem feels that her experiences there helped develop her independent spirit.

forts to bring order from chaos, though in retrospect I think they probably depressed her further."

There were a few "good periods," when Mrs. Steinem's spirited and courageous nature resurfaced. One day Gloria and Mrs. Steinem answered an ad for amateur actors. Gloria acted in the story of Noah's ark, while Ruth Steinem worked backstage creating thunder sound-effects. Gloria also tells of the night she was bitten by a rat, when her mother, "summoning cour-

age from some unknown reservoir of love," overcame her terror of leaving the house and took her to the hospital, becoming for one night the calm and comforting parent that Gloria had so longed for.

But the good periods were few and far between. There were times when Gloria knew that she and Mrs. Steinem needed help urgently, but neither mother nor daughter had any idea where to turn. Leo Steinem was on the road and could rarely, if ever, be found.

Gloria (right) shares a joke with her best friend in the summer of 1940. Within a few years, World War II's gasoline rationing would shut down the Clark Lake resort, and Gloria's father would leave home.

Susanne helped out when she could, but she was struggling too—first to get through college and then to support herself. Of Gloria's more distant relatives—grandparents, uncles, aunts— many had died, and others had apparently decided that they could not or would not do anything for Ruth Steinem, whom some saw as merely weak and self-indulgent. As for professional help, Gloria's one early brush with psychiatrists scared her away for the rest of her childhood:

> One hot and desperate summer between the sixth and seventh grade, I finally persuaded [my mother] to let me take her to the only doctor from the sanatorium days whom she remembered without fear. Yes, the brusque old man told me after talking to my abstracted, timid mother for twenty minutes: She definitely belongs in a state hospital. I should put her there right away. But even at that age, *Life* magazine and newspaper exposés had told me what horrors went on inside those hospitals. Assuming there to be no other alternative, I took her home and never tried again.

Gloria sought escape through reading. Every week she went to the library, took out three books, and lost herself in stories of other times and places. She read *Gone With the Wind* and *Little Women* over and over. Sometimes she fantasized that she was really adopted, and that soon her real family would come and tell her that the years in East Toledo were all some terrible mistake.

She would tell herself that she was not like the other kids in her neighborhood, that they might be here forever, but she was only passing through. As soon as she was old enough, she would leave town.

Her plan was to dance her way out of Toledo. Like her father, she had dreams of show business. She also had some talent; the cigarette girl at the Clark Lake resort had taught her to tap dance, and by the time she was 9 or 10 she was dancing in public. In high school, she earned $10 a night for tap dancing in a local revue. She would dance anywhere—supermarket openings, local operettas, parties at the Eagles Club. Tall, dark-haired Gloria was able to pass for 16 when she was 12. Three years later she pretended to be 21 in order to enter talent contests. The money she earned came in very handy, of course; and the costumes and makeup helped her imagine a brighter, larger world. She told herself that someday she would be a Rockette, one of the famous chorus-line dancers at the Radio City Music Hall in New York. She would live among people who understood her, loved books as much as she did, and went to the best theaters and elegant restaurants. She would marry Mr. Right and never go without heat or see a rat again.

In the meantime, she danced, read her library books, and made friends among her fellow tap dancers and

Gloria Steinem plays the piano in 1945. She often dreamed that her musical and dancing talents would enable her to escape her troubled life in Toledo.

Gloria (right) poses with friends at a Michigan Girl Scout camp in 1946. Camp provided her with a much-needed break from her responsibilities in Ohio.

classmates at her enormous Toledo high school. She and her friends would double-date at parties and stock-car races. She had her first single date, with her dancing partner, when she was about 15. It was not a success. Steinem later wrote that she had always felt at ease with him until the night of their date, when she remembers being stricken "with this terrible, sweaty-palmed insecurity, just awful—not knowing how to act, not knowing if you could excuse yourself to go to the ladies' room or not."

When Gloria finally did escape Toledo, her deliverance took a far more humdrum route than a job with the Rockettes: Her sister Susanne, now in her twenties, convinced their father that Gloria deserved one last year of normal high-school experience. Leo and Ruth Steinem had divorced by now, but he agreed to bring his ex-wife to California and care for her for a year. Gloria went to live with her older sister in Washington, D.C., and finished high school there. The move marked the beginning of a new, much happier life.

It took Steinem a long time to recover fully from the days in East Toledo. "For years and years and years," she wrote on her 50th birthday, "I would pass any slum dwelling or ramshackle house in the country and imagine I would end up living there." But she remembers both her parents with affection and gratitude. Her book of collected writings, *Outrageous Acts and Everyday Rebellions*, is dedicated in part to her father, "who taught me to love and live with insecurity"; and to her mother, "who performed the miracle of loving others even when she could not love herself."

The 1952 yearbook of Western High School in Washington, D.C., included a smiling portrait of Gloria Steinem.

THREE

The Education of an Activist Writer

The year Gloria Steinem spent with her sister in Washington, D.C., was a thrilling change for her. At last she was in an orderly, well-kept household, free of the constant worry about her mother's health and safety. "Washington was a whole new world of people who sat down to eat at regular hours," Steinem later recalled. "Nobody ate standing up out of the refrigerator. People took naps. There were boys who read books." She was exhilarated to learn that there were men in the world such as her sister's friends, who had the time and inclination to discuss politics, art, and literature. Until then, she had always believed that serious grown-up men only thought about "important things," such as how to get the bills paid on time.

Gloria lived in a house her sister rented with friends and attended the local high school. With her sister's help, she began planning for college. (Susanne Steinem had shared Gloria's desire to escape Toledo, writing away for a Smith College catalog when she was only in the third grade.) Unsurprisingly, Gloria had never learned good study habits, and her school record was poor. But she did brilliantly on her College Board exams and was accepted at Smith, one of the prestigious "Seven Sisters" women's colleges that were then considered the female counterparts of the virtually all-male Ivy League schools.

When Mrs. Steinem learned of Gloria's acceptance at Smith, she sold the East Toledo house for $8,000 to help pay the tuition. The house, such as it was, was Mrs. Steinem's only home, but she was determined to give her daughter the independent college ex-

Smith College students consult a map of Paris during a semester abroad. Steinem spent her junior year studying in Geneva, Switzerland.

perience she herself had never had.

Steinem was thoroughly content at Smith. Although in later years she came to regret the conventional attitudes she absorbed at college, at the time she "couldn't understand the women who were not happy there. They gave you three meals a day to eat, and all the books you wanted to read—what more could you want?" Hoping that her Smith education would liberate her from the limitations of her background in working-class Toledo, Steinem wholeheartedly embraced the college life and, for the time being, adapted to Smith's social and academic standards.

She was a great success socially. Friends were drawn to her because of her warmth, liveliness, and ability to listen. In some ways, she was far more mature than many of her classmates—after all, she had been coping with adult problems since the age of 10. But in matters of style and appearance, at least, Steinem was anxious to be as much like her fellow students as possible. A pretty young woman—still dark-haired then and just getting over her childhood plumpness—she did not *feel* especially attractive. Nor was she out to set any trends. "In college," she once said, "I was still trying to conform by figuring out what I was supposed to be and being it."

Her main academic interests were writing and political science. Ever since she could remember, she had wanted to be a writer, but she assumed it was impossible. She had never met anyone, male or female, who made a living by writing, and she "didn't see any women out there in the world who were professional journalists"—which was ironic, considering that her own mother had been a successful journalist before Steinem was born. She did take a creative writing course, but she was put off by the intellectual stories most students wrote, with little plot and less heart.

She decided to major in government, which was an act of mild rebellion at a time when many young women were still encouraged to study art or literature and leave serious political analysis to men. Nevertheless, Steinem was drawn to the study of political science, especially foreign policy. She spent her junior year in Geneva, Switzerland, where she learned about European politics. For her senior thesis, she combined her political and literary interests by writing about two men whose careers had involved both areas—George Orwell (author of *1984* and *Animal Farm*) and Arthur Koestler (author of *Darkness at Noon*). Like Orwell and Koestler—and, indeed, like many Western intellectuals during the period of heightened U.S.–Soviet tensions known as the cold war era—Steinem was a fervent anticommunist.

A political liberal, she preferred the Democratic party to the Republican because she believed it spoke more strongly for the underdog. Since earliest childhood she had identified with society's have-nots and second-class citizens. She had always been greatly upset by stories about the oppression of the less fortunate. She remembers crying for hours when she read a scene in Fyodor Dostoyevski's *Crime and Punishment* in which a worn-out horse is cruelly beaten. Steinem's many achievements in college did not lessen this sense of sympathy and identification with those that society often ignores or forgets.

Steinem was elected to Phi Beta

Gloria Steinem's graduation photo from the Smith College yearbook. Although many young women were encouraged to study literature and art in the 1950s, Steinem majored in government.

Kappa, the national honor society for outstanding college students. She also won a scholarship to help pay her tuition, graduated from Smith *magna cum laude* (with high honors), and was offered a postgraduate fellowship to study in India for two more years.

One thing that Steinem appreciated about all-women's colleges such as Smith was the large number of female professors and role models. Two brilliant professors who influenced her—a Shakespeare scholar and a foreign-policy expert—were both women. Steinem also liked being able to speak her mind in class without being made to feel like "a female misfit in a mostly male classroom, the fate of so many women in coed schools." Still, although she could not put this into words until years later, she was troubled by the mixed message Smith conveyed to its students in the 1950s: Smith women were encouraged to work hard and to seek excellence on their own, but were then expected to get married and "subordinate themselves to children and their husbands' careers." Steinem fully intended to get married one day but was in no hurry. If getting married meant substituting her husband's goals and ideas for her own—and she knew of no other kind of marriage—then it was a frightening prospect.

During her Smith years Steinem dated often. In the beginning of her senior year, she went to New York for the weekend and met a young newspaperman on a blind date. He recalls that she did a tap dance—"She was a helluva dancer"—and that they played word games at dinner. He was smitten. For the next few months he visited her on weekends, and sometimes he would rent a plane, fly over her dormitory, and write her name in the sky. That spring he asked her to marry him. She agreed at first, but she could not bring herself to go through with it. Finally, as he recounts it, he woke up one morning and found her engagement ring on his pillow with a note saying, "I'm sorry."

Steinem was 19 or 20 years old before she had any sexual experience beyond hugging and kissing. In this she was unlike many of her friends from her Toledo days, who had gotten pregnant during high school and "had to get married"—which, Steinem explained recently to an interviewer, was considered "okay because they had only slept with this one person whom they married.... It was made very clear to me that there were just two kinds of girls: nice girls and bad girls. [Being] a quote bad girl unquote meant sleeping with somebody you didn't subsequently marry." "Bad girls" might be shunned; their families were disgraced. While she was growing up, Steinem recalls that she made very sure she "was in the 'nice girl' category." But soon after her graduation from Smith, she found that she was pregnant.

She was terrified. Her boyfriend wanted her to give up her fellowship to India and to settle down right away. But she did not want to marry him, and she did not want to have a child—not then, at least, when her life as an independent individual was just beginning after all those years of caring for her mother. Feeling that a new trap was closing in around her just as she was leaving another behind, Steinem

Gloria Steinem (second row, sixth from left) and some of her classmates line up outside their dormitory on the Smith College campus.

became desperate and even thought of suicide. Finally Steinem decided that she had no choice but to get an abortion, which was illegal in the United States at that time. She had heard about secret "back-alley" abortions and the women who had died or been injured for life as a result of them. Knowing of no reputable physician who would perform an illegal abortion in this country, she fled to Great Britain, where abortions were legal.

Steinem flew off to England alone, feeling like a criminal. Except for two doctors whose consent was required by law, she told no one about her pregnancy or her plans to have an abortion. It was more than a dozen years before she could bring herself to discuss this sad and, as it then seemed, shameful episode in her life. Later on, the issue of abortion would draw her into the women's movement.

Soon after the abortion Steinem

went to India. Her two-year fellowship could not have come at a better time. It took her half a world away from the man she had refused to marry and the friends in whom she had not dared to confide. Of course, she had not originally applied to go to India for these reasons. At 22, Steinem wanted to expand her world, and chose India in particular because it had fascinated her since childhood. Indian religious thought had also been familiar since her earliest years: Both her mother and grandmother had been theosophists, members of a religious sect with close ties to mystical Eastern religions, especially those of India.

India is the second most populous country in the world and one of the poorest. When Steinem arrived there in 1956, the country was still feeling aftershocks of its successful struggle for independence from England, which became official in early 1950. Boundaries were in dispute; religious factions were locked in bitter struggle. The nation was reeling from recent violence, including the 1948 assassination of Mahatma Gandhi, the great proponent of nonviolent civil disobedience who had led India's independence movement. Despite laws against it, India's ancient caste system—in which people were assigned at birth to rigid, permanent roles in society—still held sway in many parts of the country. To a recent graduate of privileged, ladylike Smith

A Hindu holy man performs an ancient funeral ritual in Calcutta, India. Even before her trip, Steinem had been fascinated by Indian philosophy and religion.

College, everyday life in India must have been a revelation.

Steinem took to the country immediately and immersed herself in Indian life. She lived with Indian families and even dressed in the *saris*—long pieces of fabric that are wound around the body—worn by Indian women. (Wearing native dress showed Steinem how standards of female propriety vary from one place and time to another. "Till then," she recalled, "I'd never exposed my midriff. In that society, I found my sense of modesty got transferred from my midriff to my legs.") Steinem's fellowship included coursework at universities in New Delhi and Calcutta, but she soon lost interest in her classes, deciding she could learn a great deal more by experiencing India firsthand.

She became active in Indian politics and traveled around the country. At one point she found herself in southern India at a time when people there were rioting against the caste system. During these protests, Steinem began keeping a diary, hoping that she might someday sell her writing in the United States and inform Americans of the terrible poverty and violence that were commonplace in India. Steinem was recruited to join peacemaking teams that traveled from village to village,

Observing the differences between standards of dress for American and Indian women, Steinem began to see how subjective — and arbitrary — social codes can be.

Bricks hold down the roofs in this New Delhi slum. The suffering and poverty that Steinem witnessed during her two years in India fueled her desire to work for social justice.

wherever they were needed. Although quite obviously a foreigner, she traveled freely and safely, and people talked and listened to her. She found that "a white woman is less threatening than a white man" in other cultures, and could therefore often win the confidence of those who might be suspicious of a foreign man.

Following a pattern that she had begun during college and would continue throughout her life, Steinem tried to combine political activism with freelance writing. She wrote articles for Indian newspapers from an outsider's point of view. In most cases she found that her writing assignments concerned less serious, more "feminine" issues than her political work—another pattern that, to her increasing frustration, would persist for many years. Steinem also wrote a guidebook for the Indian government. *The Thousand Indias*, as it was called, was designed to tell visitors about many aspects of the country they would miss if they limited themselves to the usual tourist attractions.

India exposed Steinem to poverty on a scale she had never—not even in her worst days in Toledo—believed existed. For the woman who had cried at

the horse-beating scene in *Crime and Punishment*, this firsthand knowledge of such vast human suffering was a lesson never to be forgotten. America's standard of living was not the world's. After her visit to India, the United States seemed like "an enormous frosted cupcake in the middle of millions of starving poor."

Steinem also decided that the prevailing American wisdom—whether about midriffs or global politics—should not be accepted without question. She discovered, for instance, that the Vietnamese leader Ho Chi Minh, almost always spoken of as a vicious enemy of freedom in the American press, was considered the George Washington of his people by millions of Vietnamese and was respected in many other parts of the world.

Steinem returned to the United States in 1958. When asked in later life to state the most important lessons of her youth, she replied, "Learning two things: how much I had to learn, and that there were many others who knew even less. Without that second part of the realization, especially finding out that the establishment isn't as smart as its publicity would have us believe, I wouldn't have been able to act."

Steinem returned home from India determined to make Americans more aware of international issues and sought a job in television or publishing. Sexism and the era's conservative political climate thwarted her crusade.

FOUR

Starting Out

When Steinem returned home from India in 1958, she was a young woman with a mission: to make Americans aware of what was going on in Asia. She arrived in New York determined to get her message across, applying for jobs in television and, when that failed, magazines. The answer was always the same: She could be a secretary if she wanted, perhaps even a researcher. Despite her fine college record and writing experience abroad, nobody wanted a woman writer. Steinem also began to suspect that, even had she been a man, the complacent America of the late 1950s would not have been terribly interested in hearing about world problems. As Steinem later wrote, "I . . . had come back feeling as if I'd discovered poverty in the world, and when I'd talk about it, people started nodding off."

Finally she took a job in Cambridge, Massachusetts, with a foundation called Independent Research Service,

an offshoot of the politically liberal National Student Association. One of her duties was to recruit American students for Soviet-sponsored international youth festivals. The festivals, which were held in Europe, tried to promote understanding among students from countries with different forms of government.

In 1960, while Steinem was working for the Independent Research Service, John F. Kennedy was elected president. She had worked on his campaign and was a staunch supporter. She considered him a cultured man and a fellow idealist, a president who shared her sense that Americans should see themselves as part of the world around them. As she later wrote, the Kennedy era made her feel "connected to the government. For writers, it was the only time we felt that something we wrote might be read in the White House."

In this climate of new hope and ide-

Disappointed by the conservatism of the 1950s, Steinem was heartened by John F. Kennedy's 1960 election to the presidency. A new period of political idealism had begun.

alism, Steinem moved to New York to establish a career in journalism. She found an apartment with her friend Barbara Nessim, a painter. Neither woman had much money, so they chose a one-room, fourth-floor walk-up apartment in Manhattan. They managed to get a little privacy by dividing the room in half and putting their beds at opposite ends.

Once again, Steinem went out looking for a writing job. She soon found one, at a humor magazine called *Help!*

but it was hardly the job of her dreams. *Help!* specialized in political satire and was run by the former editor of *Mad* magazine. As one of a staff of three, Steinem wrote photo captions, did odd jobs, and tried to convince celebrities to appear on the magazine's cover.

Steinem had great success persuading famous people to cooperate with *Help!* Her editor remembers that "Gloria, starting from absolute scratch, not knowing anybody, would line them up. She would just pick up the phone and talk to people and charm them out of the trees." He adds, "I was probably in love with her back then, along with everybody else."

Another account of Steinem during her early days as a writer—this from entertainment reporter Liz Smith—is somewhat different. Smith and her old friend from college, Bob Benton, used to get together often in New York. "When we'd meet," Smith says, "Benton always brought this mousy, bespectacled girl along. I wondered what a bright art director saw in a girl like that. She seldom spoke, and was too shy to join in the exhibitionism that passed among us for dancing." Still, Smith liked Steinem and offered to help her rise in the world of celebrity reporting. Steinem showed no interest in the offer, and so Smith "dismissed her as not quite bright." Years later, when Smith saw a glamorous, long-haired woman modeling at a charity fashion show, she did not even recognize Steinem.

Steinem herself recalls being "serious and academic"—not much fun—during those early years. After all, success at school and hard work had enabled her to escape the slums of Toledo. Steinem hoped that by dressing plainly and acting serious, she would be treated like a respected professional.

At *Help!*, Steinem learned the nuts and bolts of putting out a magazine.

She also began to make contacts with people who could help her find freelance writing jobs. In 1961 and early 1962 she got a few assignments—short, unsigned pieces, and none on the subjects she thought really mattered. Many of her earliest assignments were for *Esquire*, where her friend Bob Benton then worked. At times she wondered whether there was any point in doing these anonymous minor pieces, but Benton and others convinced her that she had to start somewhere, and they reassured her that she was a talented writer with valuable ideas.

Steinem and Benton, who later became a distinguished screenwriter, came very close to getting married. They even took out a marriage license. Their engagement did not so much break off as peter out. They dawdled over getting the blood tests, then waited a while longer to get the ring. Steinem never seemed to find the time to buy her wedding dress—and then one day she got a form letter saying that the marriage license had expired. As with almost all her romantic attachments, this one ended amicably, slipping into a calmer, more enduring friendship. More than 20 years after their engagement, Steinem wrote of him as the man "whose long-ago listening to stories of a Toledo childhood helped show me that I needn't be someone else to be a writer."

In 1962 Steinem's first major signed

Visiting Toledo in the early 1960s, Steinem shares a quiet moment with her aunt (top left), her mother (right), and her great-aunt.

article, "The Moral Disarmament of Betty Coed," was published in *Esquire*. In it she explored how birth-control pills and other readily available contraceptives were changing sexual attitudes on U.S. college campuses. Her interviews with college students confirmed what most Americans suspected: that sex before marriage was becoming more common, and more acceptable, among college women now that it was easier to prevent unwanted pregnancies. What made Steinem's article original was her analysis of how this supposed "freedom" was harmful to many young women. The problem, she argued, was that college women who had once expected to become full-time wives and mothers soon after graduation were now being pressured into affairs—and dead-end jobs—they did not really want. The "contraceptive revolution" was forcing women to change their roles, but without any change in men's basic attitudes. Young women were no longer saying no to sex without marriage and children but had so far gained very little in return.

The *Esquire* article was well received and began to attract meaty assignments from other editors. But a few months later Steinem made what she later called a grave professional mistake: She took an assignment from the now-defunct *Show* magazine to work as a Playboy "Bunny" and write an ex-

posé of the New York Playboy Club. Her two-part article, called "A Bunny's Tale," brought her enormous attention, but it was the kind of attention a serious female journalist in 1963 did not need.

Playboy Bunnies were young women who worked waiting tables, taking photos, checking coats, and otherwise serving guests at the many clubs owned by Hugh Hefner, publisher of *Playboy* magazine. Dressed in high heels, white rabbit ears, and scanty swimsuit-type uniforms with push-up bras and tufted cotton tails, Bunnies were supposed to exemplify what men most desired in women. According to Playboy, being a Bunny was "the top job in the country for a young girl." The ad Steinem brought with her to apply for a Bunny job read:

GIRLS:
  Do Playboy Club Bunnies Really
  Have Glamorous Jobs,
  Meet Celebrities, And
  Make Top Money?

Steinem very much doubted it. Armed with a fake name, age, and identity—Marie Ochs, aged 24, college dropout and sometime beachcomber and "hostess dancer"—Steinem set out to infiltrate the Playboy Club and find out what working there was really like.

Getting the job was easy. Steinem's looks made the grade, and her job interviewers weren't interested in much else. At first Steinem worried that her

Flanked by her children, a New York woman displays a message to Pope Paul VI following the pontiff's 1968 condemnation of birth control. A few years before, Steinem had written an article pointing out that many of the attitudes that went along with readily available contraception could be harmful to women.

"Bunny Mother," as supervisors were called, might trip her up about Marie Ochs's history; but she barely glanced at Steinem's application. "We don't like our girls to have any background," she said. "We just want you to fit the Bunny image." Steinem was taken to a wardrobe mistress, who squeezed her into a satin costume so tight she could hardly breathe, then stuffed an entire plastic dry-cleaning bag into the top of it. The Bunny Mother liked what she saw, and Steinem was hired.

Steinem was told that before she could start work she would have to undergo a medical exam by the Playboy Club's doctor, including a venereal disease test and an internal physical. When she got to the doctor's office, Steinem told him that she objected to being put through these tests. He implied that the V.D. test was required by law for waitresses, and pressured her into going through with the internal exam as well. Later that day she called the Board of Health and was told that the city did not require any medical tests at all for waitresses.

For the next three weeks Steinem went through training, checked coats, and waited tables. During that time she learned how to walk, talk, dress, and act like a Bunny. Her supervisors and her job manual—called the "Bunny bible"—provided detailed instructions on everything from facial expressions (smile at all times) to Playboy-approved responses to problems that might arise with customers. Steinem was taught to say "Sir, you are not allowed to touch the Bunnies" and "Sorry, we're unable to take ladies' coats." Playboy even hired a detective agency to report on Bunny dress, attitude, dating habits, and obedience to Playboy rules. For each infraction—a dirty tail, stockings with a run, a face too pale, heels too low—Bunnies were assigned "demerits," fines that reduced their salaries. Steinem soon discovered that Bunnies were also overworked, underpaid, given almost inedible food to eat, and misled about the amount of tips they could expect.

Women employees surround Playboy *magazine publisher Hugh Hefner. Steinem said she thought Hefner wanted "to go down in history" as a man of sophistication. "But," she added, "the last person I would want to go down in history as is Hugh Hefner."*

Steinem was not impressed by the caliber of Playboy's male customers. By and large, she saw them as unattractive, boorish, and pathetic—so much for glamour! Customers pawed at the Bunnies and propositioned them constantly. "If you're my Bunny," they would say, "does that mean I can take you home?" In theory, Bunnies were not allowed to date customers. One of the detective agency's jobs was to catch Bunnies who made arrangements to meet customers outside the club. If caught, a Bunny could be fired. However, Steinem soon discovered that certain preferred customers were treated differently. Bunnies, she would later write, were not only allowed to date these "Number One Keyholders" and their friends, but had sometimes been fired for refusing.

"Marie Ochs" never was found out. There was one close call, when a couple who knew Steinem well came to the club, but they didn't recognize her behind her heavy makeup and required three-quarter-inch false eyelashes. Finally Steinem concocted a story about a family illness and quit. By then her muscles ached, her body was marked by her tight-fitting costume, and her feet were permanently enlarged a half-size from working long shifts in very high heels.

Steinem's Bunny article caused a sensation. Unfortunately, most people who read it did not focus on its often-hilarious satire or its telling criticisms of the Playboy Club. They thought of it as a sexy story. Editors typecast her as a "lightweight," and she was not offered the opportunity to work on serious topics, such as politics. To many, Steinem became "that girl who worked as a Bunny." She would cringe when people made jokes about her at parties or introduced her, without explanation, as a former Bunny. She became

Wearing her Bunny suit, Steinem carries a tray of drinks at the Playboy Club. She later wrote a stinging exposé of the club's exploitation of its women workers.

the steady object of obscene telephone threats. For a while it seemed as if nobody remembered anything else about her, or even that she had only taken the Bunny job because of a writing assignment.

One person who took her article seriously—at least seriously enough to retaliate—was Hugh Hefner, Playboy's president. For years afterward, Hefner would embarrass Steinem by publishing her Bunny publicity photos in *Playboy* magazine. According to Steinem, her picture was published "amid ever more pornographic photos of other Bunnies." Playboy Enterprises also sued Steinem for libel, but the allegations against her were eventually dropped.

Still, some good did come out of "A Bunny's Tale." As an immediate result of her article, Hugh Hefner stopped requiring physical exams for Bunnies. State authorities also used Steinem's testimony as part of a case against Playboy for violating liquor laws. The case came to nothing at the time, but Playboy was later denied an Atlantic City casino license partly because of this investigation.

In 1970, Steinem interviewed Hefner for *McCall's* magazine. By this time she had become a self-confident feminist who believed that "all women are Bunnies" in a male-dominated society. In her article, she exposed the Playboy empire, pointing out to Hefner that his Playboy Enterprises had "made women objects, more easily exchanged than sports cars." She also had these adjectives for the Playboy point of view: "boyish, undeveloped, antisensual, vicarious, and sad." In 1985, "A Bunny's Tale" was made into a TV movie. For years Steinem had resisted the idea of dramatizing her article, afraid of an-

Publisher Hugh Hefner once rejected a Playboy *piece on the women's movement for being too "well balanced," pointing out that "these chicks are our natural enemies."*

other round of sex jokes and ridicule. But this time around, Steinem's story was produced in a spirit of serious feminism and accepted as such by most viewers. The year 1986 finally saw the end of the Bunnies: In June Playboy Enterprises closed its last three clubs in the United States, due to financial failure.

A successful writer by the early 1960s, Steinem still had difficulty obtaining assignments on the political and social issues she wanted to address.

FIVE

A Double Life

In 1963, the same year "A Bunny's Tale" appeared, Steinem published *The Beach Book*, a lighthearted volume for sun-worshipers. It includes more than 80 pages on "The Suntan." The book also contains paintings of the seashore, poems and fiction about the beach and the ocean, word games and quizzes, even instructions on how to make a bikini.

The publication of *The Beach Book* demonstrated how much Steinem's life had changed since she came to New York to start her career as a free-lancer. Three years earlier, she had sometimes despaired of ever getting a signed writing assignment; now Viking, the distinguished New York publisher, had released a book under her name. Three years ago she had known almost no one in literary or celebrity circles; now some of the most respected and talented people in New York had contributed to *The Beach Book*. John Kenneth Galbraith, the brilliant economist, wrote the book's introduction, saying that he really did not especially care for the beach, but did "like this book and the girl who put it together." Steinem was adapting well to high-powered life in New York, associating with the influential and famous and on her way to becoming famous and influential herself.

But what had happened to the crusading zeal she brought home with her from India? Steinem had planned to write about world poverty, not witty fantasies about meeting Cary Grant on the beach. Would she ever manage to shake the Bunny image—and was her image as the author of *The Beach Book* really any closer to what she wanted to be? India and all it had meant to her had no relation to her stylish new life. After a while her experience in India became like a dream, leaving her with a sense of loss and frustration she did not herself understand at the time.

The early 1960s brought Steinem two

Economist John Kenneth Galbraith (center) and President John F. Kennedy (left) greet Indian prime minister Jawaharlal Nehru in 1961. Some observers expressed surprise when the distinguished Galbraith wrote the introduction to Steinem's whimsical Beach Book.

A mounted escort leads the procession bearing President John F. Kennedy's body to Arlington National Cemetery in 1963.

other losses. In 1962, her father was killed in a car accident. Although he had played little direct part in her life for almost 20 years, she mourned him deeply. A year later she was jolted by the assassination of one of her idols, President John F. Kennedy, in Dallas. On the day Kennedy flew to Texas, Steinem had been in the White House, helping a friend write jokes for the president to include in his speech. She never forgot her last image of Kennedy as he walked across the White House lawn to get into his helicopter. His death made her feel as if the future had died; the ideals of her India days seemed more distant than ever.

But Steinem kept working hard at her writing. Even when she found her assignments trivial or silly, she loved her chosen profession. During the next few years she free-lanced for five or six publications and was a contributing editor to *Glamour* magazine, where she dispensed advice on popular culture, food, and style. She reached what she later termed "probably the low point in my writing life" when she wrote a long, painstakingly researched article on textured stockings for the *New York Times Magazine*. In 1964 and 1965 she also wrote for "That Was the Week That Was," a satirical television show. In her TV work and in many of her articles, Steinem developed her strong talent for humorous writing. She found that sometimes she could use humor as a gentle, indirect way of making important points about politics and society—but she would have preferred that editors let her make these points directly.

Steinem also became well known for her published interviews with actors, singers, designers, and other "beautiful people." Most of the time she found these celebrity profiles as frivolous as her other free-lance assignments. Still, she did sometimes fight to do thoughtful profiles of women she admired— Pauline Frederick, for instance, a noted TV news correspondent who Steinem thought might have become a top newscaster "if she had been a man and thus allowed to age on camera." When given a chance, Steinem chose authors as profile subjects, hoping that interviewing them might help her learn how

American writer James Baldwin, shown here at a French café in 1985, was the subject of one of Steinem's celebrity profiles. She identified, she said, with Baldwin's "sense of outrage and vulnerability."

to become a better writer herself. She covered James Baldwin, Saul Bellow, and Truman Capote—all novelists who had written about how it felt to be an outsider, and whose books had touched her for that reason. One of the few women writers she was assigned to profile was Dorothy Parker, the great short-story writer, poet, and wit.

Steinem's writing and personal style soon made her part of the celebrity set she wrote about. The plainly dressed fledgling journalist of the early 1960s had become a "dashing girl-about-

Writer and wit Dorothy Parker was another of Steinem's interview subjects. She once quipped, "I require only three things of a man. He must be handsome, ruthless, and stupid."

Sargent, saxophonist Paul Desmond, and Tom Guinzberg, president of Viking Press. But Steinem still was not ready for marriage. "Not right now," she kept telling herself. "Maybe a year or two from now."

In the meantime, Steinem's career was becoming more and more important to her. By 1965 she was making a living as a full-time writer. Despite its frustrations, she reveled in the free-lancer's life. Writing was the only thing that seemed worthwhile to her. When asked in November of that year to explain what she liked about being a writer, she said that writing itself—actually putting the words on paper—was very hard, but writing was the only occupation she had worked at that met her three criteria for a worthwhile career: "(1) When I'm doing it, I don't feel that I should be doing something else instead; (2) it produces a sense of accomplishment and, once in a while, pride; and (3) it's frightening."

Steinem meant it when she wrote that she liked a "frightening" career. Like her father before her, she loved to face the challenges of the unknown. "I can stand anything today," he used to tell her, "as long as I don't know what tomorrow might bring." As a free-lance writer, Steinem never knew what assignment she would get from one month to the next, what cities she would visit, what new people she would meet, or whether she would

town in miniskirts and gleaming white boots," an admired and envied member of that decade's "pop culture." Although her writing career sometimes seemed to be stagnating, her social life was dazzling. During those years Steinem was still looking, or half-looking, for the right husband. She had not shaken her belief that after marriage her own life would basically be a reflection of her husband's—so she sought out men whose lives were interesting and exciting. She dated film director Mike Nichols, playwright Herb make plenty of money or none at all. This sort of life suited her much better than a steady nine-to-five job. As in her romantic life, Steinem chose freedom over predictability.

As the 1960s progressed, Steinem was becoming an increasingly committed social activist, yet her political and writing lives were moving in opposite directions. Steinem the activist was rediscovering the values of international compassion she had learned in India, but Steinem the writer was still the New York "woman-on-the-go" who wrote about celebrities and style. The same year she wrote about those expensive textured stockings for the *New York Times*, she was also working to raise bail and collect old clothes for poverty-stricken migrant workers on Long Island. At the same time she was getting photographed with the trendy celebrities she profiled, Steinem was paying $62.50 a month for her walk-up apartment and having her credit card repossessed because she had used it to charge the expenses of a Mexican-American farmworkers' protest march. Steinem accompanied her friend César Chávez on this march to the Mexican border in 110-degree heat, helping him get press coverage for the farmworkers' plight. But her writing assignments during that period were on subjects such as tropical vacations for the weary New York professional.

Steinem's political sympathies oc-

Radical activist Angela Davis addresses a protest meeting in 1969. A few years earlier, Steinem had been fired from a job at Seventeen *magazine for supporting Davis.*

casionally hurt her professional life. She worked on behalf of Angela Davis, a black professor with leftist views who had been accused of aiding in the prison escape of another black radical. When the publisher of *Seventeen* magazine heard about Steinem's work for Davis, he fired her from her consultant's job there.

It was not until 1968, when *New York* magazine was founded, that Steinem's work as a writer began to reflect her personal interests and political beliefs. Steinem was one of *New York*'s cofounders; its editor was Clay Felker, a longtime colleague who would later sponsor *Ms.* magazine. Steinem became a contributing editor and regular

As Congresswoman Bella Abzug applauds his speech, Senator George McGovern greets Steinem at a women's caucus in Miami Beach. McGovern was Steinem's choice for the Democratic presidential nomination in 1968.

political columnist for *New York*. Steinem later said that it was during this period that she "felt like a reporter for the first time." No more textured stockings: Steinem wrote about peace rallies, malnutrition in the South Bronx, political campaigns, neighbor-

hood struggles for decent day-care centers, and the plight of returning Vietnam veterans.

Her new job took Steinem all over the city. When the great civil rights leader, Dr. Martin Luther King, Jr., was murdered on April 4, 1968, Felker called

Members of the "Women's Strike for Peace" gather at the Pentagon in 1967 to protest U.S. involvement in Vietnam. Steinem was a member of the antiwar movement.

Steinem and said, "Get the hell up to Harlem and just talk to people." It was a difficult assignment, but an important one. For the next several days Steinem traveled across New York's sad, angry, black neighborhoods, talking and listening. In her report, she and coauthor Lloyd Weaver praised New York's citizens and mayor for averting the riots that had erupted in 40 other cities after King's assassination. But they warned New Yorkers that they would "need a lot of luck" if racial violence was to be averted in the future. Steinem and Weaver closed their story with a quote from Dr. King: "The patience of an oppressed people cannot endure forever."

Steinem also had strong opinions on the Vietnam War. She had come to believe that America's involvement in the war was strategically and morally wrong. She thought that if President Lyndon Johnson was renominated by the Democrats and then reelected, he would only get America deeper into the war. Steinem hoped that the Democrats would nominate a strong antiwar candidate instead. Senator George McGovern was her first choice; she had met him three years earlier, while visiting John Kenneth Galbraith's Vermont farm, and had been impressed by his obvious honesty and courage. But McGovern did not want to run, so Steinem and other Democrats who shared her antiwar views settled on an-

other senator, Eugene McCarthy, who had bravely opposed Johnson in early primaries and surprised the country by his strong showing.

Soon afterward, Robert Kennedy entered the race and César Chávez, the farmworkers' union leader, convinced Steinem that Kennedy was the best candidate because of his rapport with minority groups. When Kennedy was assassinated in June 1968, her hopes again centered on McCarthy. After he proved to be an uninspiring candidate, Steinem and others convinced McGovern to seek the Democratic nomination. But by this time the antiwar faction of the Democrats was in disarray. President Johnson had dropped out of the race, and the Democrats nominated his vice-president, Hubert Humphrey, who eventually lost the election to Republican candidate Richard Nixon.

Steinem also reported on the Nixon campaign. In her writing about Nixon, as in all her political writing, she did not try to hide her sympathies. "When Nixon is alone in a room," she wrote, "is there anyone there?" This straight-from-the-hip approach, along with her gift for humor and growing political savvy, made Steinem's *New York* columns both popular and persuasive. As a writer, she was becoming a force to be reckoned with.

The late 1960s were turbulent times in America, marked by student pro-

A Kent State student reacts in horror upon seeing the body of one of the four students who had been shot and killed by National Guardsmen during a 1970 antiwar rally. As the 1960s drew to a close, Steinem often wrote about the tumultuous political scene in America.

tests, racial unrest, assassinations, and police violence. The Vietnam War divided families and friends. In many ways it was a terrible time to live through. But for a journalist with a passionate interest in the issues that shook the nation, it was also an exciting time to be writing and working to change society. The two strands of Steinem's double life were coming together: After working in journalism for over a decade, she was finally able to write about the subjects that mattered to her most.

Steinem attended her first feminist meeting in 1968. She later said of the experience, "It made me understand that women are oppressed together and so have to act together."

SIX

Feminist Awakening

On a cool November night in 1968, Steinem went to a church basement in Manhattan to attend a meeting of a radical feminist group called Redstockings. At the time she was not a member of Redstockings or of any other women's rights organization. She was on assignment for *New York* magazine and planned to report on the women's liberation movement as just one issue among many. But what Steinem saw and heard that evening would change her life.

The topic of the Redstockings meeting was abortion, then illegal in the United States except in rare, extreme cases. New York State had recently held hearings to consider relaxing its antiabortion laws, but had invited 14 men and only 1 woman (a nun) to speak. Redstockings had called its own meeting in protest.

Steinem sat in the drafty basement and listened as, one by one, women stood and told their own personal experiences with illegal abortions. The women spoke of how desperate they had been for help, how terrified and helpless they had felt. One woman said her doctor told her he would perform an abortion only if she let herself be sterilized. Another woman told of being sexually attacked on the operating table. Almost all the women who spoke had been forced to risk their health, perhaps even their lives.

As she heard these stories of danger and humiliation, Steinem felt a surge of anger so strong it almost made her physically sick. It was the same kind of anger she had experienced throughout her adult life when confronted with unfairness or inequality. Steinem had wondered why she, a middle-class person—and lately a dazzling success by almost anyone's standards—had always identified with minorities and other second-class citizens. Now she began to see: As a woman, she was a second-class citizen herself.

In a flash of awareness that she later said "seemed like the sun coming up," Steinem realized how much she had in common with these feminist activists. She might be a little older than most of them, and others might consider her life more glamorous, but she felt these differences were unimportant, while the similarities were crucial. Like the Redstockings women, Steinem was angry—at getting less pay than a man for the same free-lance assignments, at stupid jokes about dumb blonds, at being asked why she did not quit writing and get married, at dozens of annoyances and injustices, large and small. And, although she still never spoke of it, Steinem remembered the abortion she herself had undergone right after college. More than 10 years had passed, but her memories of feeling criminal and alone were still vivid.

Until the night of the Redstockings meeting, Steinem had often thought that any prejudice against her as a woman was a personal problem. If she was paid less than a man, it was probably her own fault. If she was passed over for important writing assignments, it must be because she wasn't a serious enough person—after all, she had taken that Bunny assignment voluntarily—or a good enough writer. Besides, what could she do about it? Now, as she sat stock-still on a rickety folding

Campaigning for women's right to vote, suffragists distribute pamphlets in New York City in 1916. Four years later, women finally won the vote.

chair, her reporter's notes forgotten, she began to see things differently. Women were discriminated against *as a group*, she realized, like blacks and other minorities. Prejudice against women was not a personal problem, but a social problem. And there *was* something she could do about it, but not by working alone. Women must fight together to take control of their lives.

In the weeks and months that followed, Steinem went to countless meetings of the many diverse feminist groups that were springing up all over

New York (as in the rest of the country). She read every feminist book and article she could get her hands on.

Some of what she read and heard was familiar to her. She knew that American women had first organized in the 19th century and finally won the right to vote in 1920; her own grandmother had been part of that struggle. She also knew that this "first wave" of the American women's movement had dissipated after the vote was won, and that by the 1950s there were even fewer women in politics or in well-paying jobs than there had been a generation earlier. And Steinem was familiar with Betty Friedan's ground-breaking book, *The Feminine Mystique*, which was published in 1963.

Friedan's book describes the plight of middle-class homemakers who had accepted the passive ideal of womanhood portrayed in the women's magazines, only to find themselves trapped in the suburbs without rewarding work or a sense of self-worth. Friedan is seen by many as the founder of the modern American women's movement. Her book changed the lives of countless women and was an important step in the growth of the second wave of feminism in the 1960s and 1970s. But *The Feminine Mystique* did not speak to Steinem personally, because she had never married, had children, or given up her career. Steinem's own problems mirrored those of other women who

Betty Friedan (right), a founder of the National Organization for Women, joins NOW official Kathryn Clarenbach in announcing the group's adoption of a "Bill of Rights for Women in 1968."

had gone out into the working world and found trouble—job discrimination, male resentment, psychological conflicts—at every turn.

In 1966, Betty Friedan and others had founded the National Organization for Women (NOW), with the aim of bringing women "into full participation in the mainstream of American society *now* . . . in truly equal partnership with men." NOW's specific goals included legal equality for women and an end to job discrimination.

Around the same time, dozens of other feminist groups began to form. As with NOW, their members were mostly white and middle-class, but the more radical feminists tended to be

Feminists, wearing chains to represent women's unequal political status, protest outside the White House in 1969.

younger and angrier than their NOW counterparts. Many of these younger women had taken part in the civil rights or antiwar movements. As young activists, they had found that their supposedly radical male colleagues still expected the "chicks" to keep quiet at meetings or to do all the typing.

Some of these feminist groups had detailed plans for restructuring American society, believing that the milder reforms advocated by NOW were not enough. Other groups of women concentrated on understanding their own personal experiences; they would meet for "consciousness-raising ses-

sions" in which women talked about their most private concerns. The subjects could be almost anything—one woman's fear that she didn't respond sexually the way she was "supposed" to, another's funny story about talking back to her boss, or a woman's harrowing description of a rape or beating. As Steinem had done at the Redstockings meeting, the women at these sessions learned that they were not alone, that others had felt the same way and faced similar problems.

Steinem's first openly feminist article, "After Black Power, Women's Liberation" appeared in *New York* magazine in 1969. She described what some of the young feminists in New York had been doing recently. She told of the Redstockings abortion testimony, and of women dressed as witches and black-veiled brides who invaded an exhibition of bridal gowns and kitchen appliances. She also reported on a student-run college course on "women as an oppressed class." The course included a discussion of the parallel myths that had been used to justify the mistreatment of both women and blacks ("smaller brains," "childlike natures," "put on earth to support white men").

After describing these and other groups of radical feminists, Steinem made a prediction. If the younger, more radical groups could join forces with women in organizations such as NOW, she wrote, then "an alliance with the second mass movement—poor women of all colors—should be no problem." Some women's liberation groups were already working with the poor on common issues—day-care centers, job training, the problems of women and children on welfare. Steinem was convinced that if these two groups joined forces, they would have enormous power.

Steinem's article was one of the earliest reports in the mainstream press on the women's movement, and it won a coveted Penney-Missouri Journalism Award a year after it was published.

But in the meantime, Steinem was surprised and angered by the response of most of her male colleagues. Why was she writing about "women's stuff," they would ask, when she had worked so hard to get serious, important assignments? Wasn't she afraid that writing about these crazy women would ruin her reputation?

This attitude—from the same men who had never thought of cautioning her about the Bunny article—infuriated Steinem. As she later recalled: "For the first time, I began to question the honor of being the only 'girl reporter' among men, however talented and benevolent they might be. And all the suppressed anger of past experiences I had denied or tried to ignore came flooding back." Steinem was referring to innuendos that her career had been aided by her good looks, back-handed compliments that her intelligence enabled her to "think like a man," and lowered payments for her writing because women were not supposed to need the money. Her male friends' advice backfired; Steinem became even more committed to the cause of feminism.

Steinem wrote about the women's movement whenever she could. Along with several feminist pieces for her regular *New York* column, she wrote an article for *Look* magazine about the possibility of a woman president and an essay for *Time* called "What It

Gloria Steinem sits by her typewriter in 1969, the year she published her first feminist article, "After Black Power, Women's Liberation."

Would Be Like If Women Win." In her *Time* essay, she reminded readers of the ways women were discriminated against in almost every aspect of life.

The article pointed out that in many states, for instance, married women could not get credit, start a business, or even use their maiden names. Schoolgirls were brainwashed into thinking they were naturally illogical and passive. She went on to describe how—in addition to improvements in the law—schools, families, organized religion, literature, and even manners and fashion would change if society were to adopt feminist principles. The changes could be very sweeping indeed, she said, but men should not be too alarmed. On feminism and the family, for example, she wrote:

> Women's Lib is not trying to destroy the American family. A look at the statistics on divorce—plus the way old people are farmed out with strangers and young people flee the home—shows the destruction that has already been done. Liberated women are just trying to point out the disaster, and build compassionate and practical alternatives from the ruins.

She concluded this essay by saying that "If Women's Lib wins, perhaps we all do." Ironically, Steinem herself had been discriminated against by *Time*, which paid her less for this essay than it paid men for similar assignments.

To her rising frustration and dismay, Steinem soon found that the commercial magazines had little interest in articles about the women's movement. Some saw it as just another craze that would soon blow over; others did not see it as important enough to merit more than one story. Meanwhile, the women's movement quietly was growing stronger every day.

To call this new wave of feminism "the women's movement" may be misleading. There was never a single feminist organization or a set of goals or a group of leaders everyone agreed upon. Instead, feminism and feminist

Steinem confers with tennis star Billie Jean King. In a much-publicized "battle of the sexes," King defeated professional tennis player Bobby Riggs in 1973.

ideas spread all over the country and the world, and many women found their lives and perspectives changing even though they had never joined any group at all.

Steinem wanted to spread the feminist message and looked for ways to do it outside the male-dominated press. One way was to found *Ms.* magazine. Another was to conquer her fear of public speaking and focus on lecturing instead of writing. Around the same time she worked to start *Ms.*— the years from 1969 to 1974—Steinem began traveling around the country on a series of lecture tours. During this period she went to every state but Alaska. She criss-crossed America, just as she had with her father when she was a little girl, but this time she was

Abortion rights advocates stage a 1977 demonstration in New Jersey. They were protesting a proposed constitutional amendment that would have invalidated the Supreme Court's 1973 legalization of abortion.

traveling with other women, trading new ideas instead of antique furniture.

One aspect of the women's movement that troubled Steinem was the way in which many people saw feminism exclusively as a white, middle-class issue. Steinem believed that the movement's strength and beauty lay in its potential to win respect for all women, regardless of color or background. Many of her friends and activist colleagues were black women. (Her male companion during most of those years was also black—track star Rafer Johnson. Once again, the romance ended and turned into friendship.) To demonstrate that feminism was a movement for all women, Steinem and a black feminist friend always traveled the lecture circuit as a team.

Steinem's first partner was Dorothy Pitman Hughes, a pioneer in setting up new child-care centers for low-income working women in New York. After Hughes and her husband had a baby daughter, Hughes brought the nursing baby along. Some were skeptical of this traditional arrangement made by such nontraditional women. As Steinem remarked in her introduction to *Outrageous Acts and Everyday Rebellions*, "Dorothy was convinced that some people might suspect us of renting this baby to demonstrate the integration of children into daily life, an important part of our message. In fact, one or two people behaved as if we had somehow given birth to a baby daughter by ourselves."

After Hughes, Steinem traveled with Florynce Kennedy, the outspoken activist lawyer, and then Margaret Sloan, another activist and an impressive public speaker. Sometimes people were surprised, even offended, at the sight of a black woman and a white woman sharing a podium; but many women, especially in the South, were delighted by this symbol of unity.

Steinem and her partners went to large cities and to small, out-of-the-way towns. They spoke in union halls, gyms, and churches "filled to overflowing with women (and men) who applauded and laughed with relief at hearing the sexual politics of their own lives described out loud." The basic format rarely changed: Steinem would speak first and lay the groundwork. Then her partner—usually a more experienced public speaker, according to Steinem—would take over.

But the most important part of the talk came afterward: small all-women discussion groups and meetings to organize local feminist projects. Women in the audience would ask and answer questions about their daily lives, tell one another of local problems—a factory that refused to hire women, for instance—and pass around sign-up lists for groups that were forming in their area. Steinem would share what she had learned on her travels; at many

Initially petrified by public speaking, Steinem made appearances around the nation to spread the feminist message. She later said she learned three lessons from her years on the road: "(1) You don't die; (2) there's no right way to speak, only your way; and (3) it's worth it."

meetings, she learned as much as she taught. After most lectures, groups of women would get together for impromptu consciousness-raising sessions with Steinem and her partner. Steinem became (and has remained) legendary for her willingness to listen as well as to talk and for taking the time to follow up her public speaking engagements with smaller, more personal encounters. During her lecture tour, she would stay up late at night in her motel room, week after week, as women told their stories of being sexually harassed at work, beaten up by their husbands, or abandoned after years of marriage.

Although most of their audiences were vocal in their support of Steinem and her message, she and her partners also had to face hostility and anger. In one audience, a man screamed that

Hughes should "go home to Russia where you belong!" This particular insult only made Hughes, and the audience, burst out laughing, because as a black woman, she obviously was not of Russian extraction. Other antagonists were more frightening—such as the man who tried to storm the stage one night, screaming that all this talk of equality was "blasphemous." Steinem and her partners were heckled, ridiculed, and threatened many times, but the joy and excitement of their other listeners more than made up for the unfriendly ones.

Steinem's new life required many sacrifices. Although she officially lived in New York—by now she had moved into her two-room apartment in the East Side brownstone—there were weeks when she was lucky to spend two nights in her own home. She never got enough sleep; when she wasn't on her tour or working for *Ms.*, she was appearing on television, going to political strategy meetings for the upcoming Democratic election campaign, or trying to find a few hours for her writing. Steinem missed being able to write without interruption. She had also given up most of the glittery social life of her earlier days in New York. This was not really a sacrifice, though; that sort of life no longer appealed to her. When she had a chance to relax, she preferred to spend time at home with close friends.

There were many who wondered why Steinem had chosen to devote her life to the feminist movement. She had already made it in the man's world of print journalism before feminism came along, and she had been offered many chances to succeed in the traditional women's role of marriage and family. So what was in it for her? What more did she want?

Everything, Steinem might have said. She did not see herself as others saw her. They saw an impressive list of publications, but she saw books and articles that meant little to her and were not what she wanted to be writing. They saw a woman who had done well for herself; she knew that she could be truly happy only if she worked to better society, not just her own life. They saw a beautiful trendsetter—"One of the best dates to take to a New York party," to quote *Time* magazine in 1969—but she remembered that, before feminism came along, she had felt torn in half. She had been doubtful about her talent, terrified to speak in public, and reluctant to discuss certain aspects of her past even with close friends. Without knowing why, she had been lonely and confused. Now she felt that she had found her true vocation, and that the strands of her life—memories, friendships, politics, writing, and a passion for causes—were finally weaving together. In Steinem's opinion, feminism had saved her life.

A prochoice demonstrator (one who supports legal abortion) confronts an antiabortion, or prolife, advocate (left) outside a Boston rally.

SEVEN

Gains and Setbacks

The early 1970s were a time of enormous activity for the American feminist movement. NOW had increased its membership from 300 at its founding in 1966 to 48,000 by 1974; hundreds of smaller, more local or specialized women's groups were also forming and expanding. Women started to move into law, business, and medicine in greater numbers, and to fight actively for a larger role in other traditionally male jobs. Women rabbis, firefighters, sports stars, and construction workers were making news. The tiny number of women in political office grew slightly, and women started lobbying male politicians on women's issues. New laws were enacted, and old laws were enforced, to give women equal rights in jobs, marriage, education, credit, school athletics, and countless other areas. Congress passed the Equal Rights Amendment to the Constitution (ERA), which, if ratified by the states, would grant women "equal-

ity of rights under the law." Several states also passed their own ERAs. About a dozen states passed less strict abortion laws, and in 1973, the United States Supreme Court ruled that women had a right to choose for themselves whether or not to have an abortion. Women established shelters for battered wives and children, sued employers who used sexual threats, and fought to change rape laws that often seemed to put the victim on trial. Everywhere there were demonstrations, marches, rallies, fund-raisers, and meetings.

Even the English language changed. Terms such as *reproductive freedom* (the right to decide when and whether to bear children), *sexism*, and *male chauvinism* began to appear. Words such as *chairman* and *mailman* were discredited and replaced by such sex-neutral terms as *chair* and *letter carrier*. *Ms.* came into use, of course, and adult women were less likely to be called *girls*. Schools began to require new textbooks that would be free of sexist as well as racist stereotypes.

In addition to her lecture tours and her *Ms.* editorship, Steinem took part in many of feminism's major public events. Her rise to prominence was swift. Within less than two years, she became one of the movement's most active strategists, as well as one of the handful of women—along with Betty Friedan, writer Kate Millett, and Congresswomen Bella Abzug and Shirley Chisholm—most often cited as feminist leaders.

In 1970 she helped organize the largest women's-rights demonstration in American history: the Women's Strike for Equality. This event, held on August 26, exactly 50 years after women won the right to vote, was marked by rallies, marches, pickets, sit-ins, and lectures across the nation. The biggest rally and march was held in New York City, where Steinem, Friedan, and more than 10,000 others (some have estimated the figure to be as high as 50,000) walked down Fifth Avenue to Manhattan's Bryant Park, chanting "Liberation Now, Equality Now!" The day was beautiful and the mood euphoric. In Bryant Park, the crowd laughed, wept, and applauded as the speakers, including Friedan and Steinem, spoke of their experiences as women and exhorted their listeners to help achieve the strike's three goals: job and educational equality, free child-care, and the right to abortions for women who wanted them (this was three years before the Supreme Court's decision on abortion).

It had been hard to get the nation's many diverse women's groups to agree even on these three goals. Some women thought they went too far, and many thought they did not go far enough. But, for that day at least, unity won out over diversity. In New York, the marchers included suburban housewives, poor women from Harlem, rich and famous women, radical lesbians, moderate Republicans, elderly suffragists who had marched in "Votes for Women" parades 50 years earlier, and high school students in bell-bottom jeans. All joined together to show their pride in being women and their urgent desire for equality. The Women's Strike for Equality was an emotional high-point in many feminists' lives, Steinem's among them.

Steinem also found the time to work for change in party politics. Although she had been involved in political campaigns in the past, for the first few months of her life as a conscious feminist, Steinem had hardly given a thought to "politics" in the traditional sense: the male-controlled world of elections to national office. But she was soon caught up in a Democratic presidential primary—although this time with a new, feminist slant. Senator

Steinem participates in a 1972 demonstration calling for the revision of U.S. welfare laws. Although feminism had become her primary focus, she continued to work for a variety of social causes.

George McGovern (Steinem's favorite candidate in the 1968 presidential elections) invited Steinem to a planning meeting called by his colleague in the Senate, Abraham Ribicoff, to discuss whether McGovern should run for president in 1972. In a campaign diary she kept during those years, Steinem recalls:

> Six months ago, I would have been honored by McGovern's invitation to a "serious" (i.e., male and therefore grown-up) political meeting, but full of doubt about whether I could contribute in a "serious" (male) way. I had raised

Steinem (right) and other keynote speakers prepare to address the opening session of the National Women's Political Caucus on July 10, 1971.

as much money and done as much practical work as anyone in McGovern's last brief presidential effort and *still* had been treated like a frivolous pariah by much of McGovern's Senate staff, but I had refused to admit even to myself that this was so.

This time around, Steinem had new confidence in the value of her political work and a new sense of how unjustly she had been treated in every campaign since her days with Students for (presidential candidate Adlai) Stevenson in 1952. She also saw that she had defined "politics" very narrowly in the past, as "faraway events in Washington or Saigon or city hall." Now she believed that all power relationships in

life were "political," and therefore important. "Politics may be who's doing the dishes, or who's getting paid half the wages that a man would get for the same job, or who's expected to take roles of service and support, including in political campaigns." In this campaign, Steinem vowed to make her views known forcefully, "without hesitancy or humor." She would not accept second-class status either for herself or for women's issues.

Steinem soon would notice a big change in the way male politicians treated her. When she saw Senator McGovern at John Kenneth Galbraith's annual Vermont picnic in 1969, McGovern apologetically explained that

Shirley Chisholm, a candidate for the Democratic presidential nomination, greets supporters in 1972. Steinem supported Chisholm's bid for the nomination, which eventually went to George McGovern.

Ribicoff had cut her name from the invitation list for the meeting to plan McGovern's candidacy. "No broads," was all Ribicoff would say. McGovern related that he had explained how Steinem had written speeches, raised money, and campaigned tirelessly for Democratic candidates but Ribicoff had just repeated, "No broads."

Steinem was used to such incidents, but she was upset by McGovern's acceptance of Ribicoff's sexism. Out of all the politicians she knew in Washington, she considered McGovern "probably the best of the lot," especially because he was working to increase the number of women in politics. Steinem knew that McGovern "would never have let Ribicoff get away with saying, 'No blacks' or 'No Jews.' 'No broads' was somehow acceptable." Outraged, she decided that unless women organized and forced male politicians to take notice, basic change would never happen.

Two years later, at another Vermont weekend gathering, everything had changed. By this time, McGovern had officially declared his candidacy for the presidency, and a huge fund-raising party was planned. Steinem was asked to be one of the speakers. A few years earlier she would not have been invited—and, even if asked, would have "pled insanity or sickness rather than stand up in front of a group larger than four." But her nationwide lecture tour, and especially the help and support of her lecture partners, had relieved Steinem of her paralyzing fear of public speaking.

She did speak at the 1971 Vermont meeting, and she ended her address by praising McGovern as "the best white male candidate." Here she was alluding to her friend Shirley Chisholm, who would also have her name on the ballot at the Democratic nominating convention in 1972. Chisholm,

a member of the House of Representatives, was a relative unknown, and black and female as well. Nobody, including Chisholm herself, seriously expected her to win; her candidacy was a symbol intended to make voters and politicians aware of social issues such as discrimination against women and minorities.

Although clearly it would take time to gain their fair share of public offices, women were becoming an increasingly organized political force. After a year of planning, a group of prominent women—including Friedan, Steinem, and Congresswomen Chisholm and Abzug—held the founding meeting of the National Women's Political Caucus (NWPC) in July 1971. The caucus, which encourages and helps women to run for office and lobbies for feminist issues, has remained a powerful force to this day.

Steinem did not limit her organizing efforts to the NWPC. In 1971 she co-founded and was chairwoman of the board of the Women's Action Alliance, which supported many feminist projects while serving as a national referral network women could use to share information. During the early 1970s Steinem also helped form a coalition of women in labor unions. Later in the decade, she and her co-workers at *Ms.* created foundations and trust funds to help women in education, the arts, and other areas.

Asserting that rising prices have left American women "up the creek," Steinem and her frequent political ally, Congresswoman Bella Abzug (left), demonstrate their argument in New York City's Central Park.

During the 1972 presidential campaign (in which Democratic nominee McGovern lost to Republican incumbent Richard Nixon) Steinem played many different roles. As a journalist, she reported on the Democratic and Republican races. As an elected representative of the NWPC, she worked to make women's voices heard at the Democratic and Republican conventions, where the parties' candidates were nominated.

With support from McGovern and others, the NWPC had great success in

Feminist activist and author Betty Friedan charged that Steinem was hurting the women's movement by endorsing "radical" viewpoints that offended many Americans.

changing the makeup of the Democrats' 1972 convention. Now 40 percent of the delegates were women, as opposed to 14 percent in the 1968 convention. A woman cochaired the convention, and yet another woman's name was seriously considered as a vice-presidential nominee (paving the way, perhaps, for the nomination of Geraldine Ferraro in 1984). The party also came out officially in support of various feminist positions. As Steinem wrote in her political diary, all this was "a far cry from 1968 when most of the women were going to luncheons and fashion shows were arranged for the 'wives.'"

Steinem also ran for a slot in the New York delegation to the Democratic convention. Here she had to choose whether to run as an official delegate for McGovern or for Chisholm. It was a difficult choice: Chisholm had no realistic chance of winning, but supporting her would demonstrate clearly Steinem's belief that women and minorities were their own best political representatives. After considerable soul-searching, she decided to back Chisholm, and was defeated.

During this period Steinem became still more prominent in the mass media, reaching even greater fame as a feminist leader than she had as a journalist and as a member of New York society. She appeared on *Newsweek's* cover under a banner reading "The New Woman," and *McCall's* magazine named her Woman of the Year. *Ms.'s* founding and spectacular early success only increased her celebrity.

Although many considered Steinem a key spokeswoman for the women's movement, she came under increasing attack from other feminists. Some, notably Betty Friedan, considered themselves more moderate than Steinem and claimed that she was damaging the women's movement with her "militant" views. Friedan and her supporters felt that Steinem was hurting the movement's growth by scaring away more traditional women and men.

One bitter split arose over the issue of lesbianism. Steinem believed firmly that "straight" (heterosexual) feminists should openly support lesbians. She felt that straight women had much to learn from some of their lesbian sisters. Besides, she contended, the women's movement should welcome *all* women; excluding lesbians—or any other group—as somehow not being "real women" would be immoral and would only play into the hands of feminism's enemies. Steinem's opponents on this issue objected that, by taking a stand on lesbians, feminism would lose its mass appeal.

Steinem was also attacked by those on the other end of the feminist political spectrum. In 1975 Redstockings—the group that had sponsored the meeting that first got Steinem involved in feminism—was one of the radical organizations that accused her of being an undercover agent for the Central Intelligence Agency (CIA). These charges began when it was revealed that the National Student Association, where Steinem worked after her return from India, had received secret contributions from the CIA. Steinem indignantly denied that she had ever been a CIA agent, but has admitted that she knew about the funding. "Yes," she said recently, "we knew at the time that some of the money came from the gov-

Steinem and presidential assistant Midge Costanza sport pro-ERA buttons at a meeting of the House Judiciary Committee. Although the panel extended the ratification deadline, the amendment failed to win passage.

ernment. It hadn't any strings attached, and we thought it was a great use of government money. That was very naive."

Steinem was also criticized by other feminists for her methods and style. Betty Friedan, in particular, claimed that Steinem and her supporters had used underhanded means to take power away from Friedan and use it to promote their own political agenda, even for their own personal glory. Other feminists objected to the idea that the media had chosen a well-off, traditionally beautiful, and famous woman like Steinem as the spokeswoman for a movement that generally

Addressing a 1979 press conference, Steinem displays a Ms. *article detailing a young woman's death from an illegal abortion. The conference was held on the sixth anniversary of the Supreme Court decision that legalized abortion.*

scorned traditional female glamour, beauty, and fame.

To remarks about her looks Steinem could only respond that she was not about to "put on combat boots or cut off my hair." As for being famous, Steinem believed that her fame, at least since she became involved in feminism, was being used for a vital purpose — the advancement of the cause of women. Still, Steinem was sensitive to this criticism, and the personal attacks

hurt. It was especially galling to be resented for fame she did not always want, and for money she did not have. Steinem had no car, no stocks or bonds, no savings at all. Her salary at *Ms.* was very modest by magazine-editor standards, and, like her father before her, she showed little talent for managing what money she did have.

In April 1976, *Ms.* published an article called "Trashing—The Dark Side of Sisterhood." The piece focused on "a particularly vicious form of character assassination which has reached epidemic proportions in the Women's Liberation Movement." The author of the article charged that some women, who had not yet learned to accept themselves, felt compelled to attack stronger women out of jealousy and resentment. The article brought enormous response from readers, and *Ms.* printed a sampling of letters about the piece, including one from Steinem. Steinem wrote that "Just as men victimize the weak member of their group, women victimize the strong one." In the long run, Steinem said, the only remedy for "trashing" was to work for a world where all women could be self-confident, and so not have to attack one another. In the short run, she concluded sadly, "I know of no answer except to recognize the trasher, see that she is at least not rewarded for hurting other women, and concentrate on constructive, tangible, unifying work." Steinem spoke from experience.

The press was not slow to publicize the splits and dissatisfactions within the women's movement. Soon many commentators were also reporting that feminism was on the way out. Some observers asked whether organized feminism was still needed, now that many of the worst legal and social barriers had begun to fall. One such article, even though it concluded that advocates such as Steinem were still useful, was titled "Is Gloria Steinem Dead?" Other commentators said that the second wave of feminism had lost sight of its original goals, along with its early vigor. By 1976 articles with titles such as "Requiem for the Women's Movement" began to appear.

There was some truth to these articles. Discord had weakened the movement. Most of the smaller, radical groups, which had given feminism much of its energy and new ideas, had disbanded by the late 1970s. Women who had organized around specific goals, such as antidiscrimination laws or the repeal of laws prohibiting abortion, drifted apart once these goals were met.

At the same time, antifeminists started organizing. Women and men who had opposed equal rights or the legalization of abortion began to form efficient, well-funded lobbying groups. Among the antifeminists' main targets were national and state Equal Rights Amendments. Several states, including Steinem's and Friedan's home state of New York, voted down state ERAs. By 1975, the national ERA was also hopelessly stalled. Although polls showed that a majority of Americans favored the ERA, it failed to meet its 1982 ratification deadline, largely due to the efforts of anti-ERA activists. (Of course, Congress can always vote to start the long process all over again.)

Steinem weathered all the changes

Male and female supporters of the National Organization for Women parade through the streets of Atlantic City, New Jersey.

of the 1970s, good and bad, and continued to serve as a feminist leader and moving force at *Ms.* Except for a day or two a week devoted to speaking and fund-raising, Steinem worked at *Ms.* every day. The success of the magazine surpassed its founders' wildest hopes. Five years after its first issue hit the stands in 1972, *Ms.*'s readership was still growing. When *Ms.* began, Steinem had planned on staying for a year or two—if the magazine lasted that long. Now, as the years passed, she found to her surprise that she was working at a steady job.

Steinem's personal life also became more settled by the end of the 1970s. She was able to spend more time at home in New York, surrounded by her

close friends and co-workers. Her colleagues at *Ms.*, and the other women and men she worked with on feminist issues, became a sort of extended family. In the mid-1970s she met and fell in love with Stanley Pottinger, a lawyer then working in the Civil Rights Division of the Justice Department. Unlike most of the men she had dated in the past, Pottinger was not especially wealthy or well known—but by then, of course, Steinem had attained a strong sense of herself as a writer and feminist and no longer felt the need to seek out rich and famous men. Steinem and Pottinger remained together for nine years. During their relationship they never married and they lived in separate apartments; both of them preferred this arrangement to traditional marriage.

Another lawyer appeared in Steinem's inner circle during the 1970s. Her sister, Susanne Steinem Patch, entered law school at the age of 50. It was a courageous decision. The Patches had six children and had also made room for Ruth Steinem in their home. Even aside from her family responsibilities, starting school again at 50 was no easy matter for Patch. Steinem was proud of her sister for not letting age, much less being a woman, stand in her way. Susanne Patch is now a government lawyer in Washington.

Gloria Steinem turned 40 in 1974, within a year of her sister's 50th birthday. This event might have passed unnoticed by the press, because most people thought that Steinem was only 38. At the start of her career, well-meaning friends had taken two years off her age when writing about her. Many people, including the man Steinem was dating at the time, said it was crazy for a woman to tell her true age—so Steinem went along with the change. "It's interesting," she recalled later, "how one small lie . . . can make you feel false and terrible." On her real 40th birthday, she decided to set the public record straight. *Ms.* threw a birthday party for her, and Steinem invited the press. At the party a reporter, meaning to be complimentary, said "You don't look 40." Steinem replied, "But this is what 40 looks like. We've been lying so long, who would know?"

In the Fifth Anniversary Issue of *Ms.* in 1977, Steinem responded to gloomy reports on feminism by writing that, although women were still discriminated against, and more American women and children than ever lived in poverty, the movement itself was "bigger and healthier than ever." Media attention-getters such as pickets and marches might have died down, but now there were "more activists, more organizations, and a whole network of

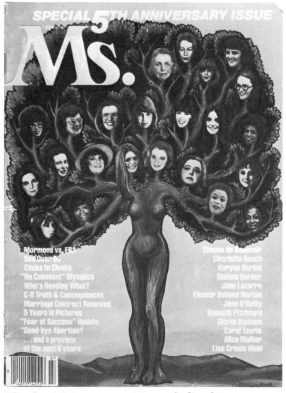

The feminist movement is symbolized as a tree on the cover of Ms.*'s Fifth Anniversary Issue. Steinem's portrait appears in the tree's branches along with those of other notable women.*

alternative feminist structures." For its anniversary cover, *Ms.* chose a tree as a symbol of feminist strength. "A tree," Steinem wrote, "that bends in the storm instead of breaking. That hibernates in cold seasons to bloom and bloom again."

Steinem, author Robin Morgan (center), and Bella Abzug (right) demonstrate against pornography, charging that it depicts women in a demeaning light.

EIGHT

Milestones

Throughout her years as a feminist leader and magazine editor, Steinem has worked steadily as a writer. Many of these articles have appeared in *Ms.*, and almost all concern women's issues. Some of Steinem's most compelling feminist articles have been about prominent women—not the "celebrity profiles" of her early writing career, but thoughtful studies of women's roles as represented by individual lives. Actually, Steinem began to write such articles even before she consciously became a feminist. In 1968, for instance, she set out to interview Richard Nixon but was granted an interview with his wife, Pat, instead. Avoiding the stereotyped image of the ever-smiling first lady so often described in the press, Steinem saw and wrote about Mrs. Nixon's early struggles against poverty and her deep resentment toward people who had always led an easy life.

In the 15 years that followed, Steinem wrote essays about prominent women such as Jacqueline Kennedy Onassis, Linda Lovelace, and Alice Walker. In each case, she tried to change her readers' perspectives on these already well-known figures by showing her subjects in a new, feminist light. For example, Steinem asked why it was that no one ever spoke about Jackie Onassis in terms of her own career as a book editor, but only as the wife of President John F. Kennedy and Aristotle Onassis. In the case of Linda Lovelace, the former pornographic movie star, Steinem wrote a chilling narrative about a woman forced by her husband into a life of fear and humiliation. Lovelace's escape from the world of pornography was to Steinem an example of "the way in which women survive—and fight back." In her Alice Walker article, Steinem praised Walker's magnificent fiction about black America and went on to attack white male literary norms, which she felt denied Walker the recognition she deserved. (Walker has

Steinem chats with Jacqueline Kennedy Onassis at the Academy of Arts and Letters. Steinem wrote an essay noting that the media emphasized Onassis's famous husbands, giving little attention to her personal accomplishments.

since won a Pulitzer Prize for her novel *The Color Purple*.)

Steinem has also written essays on such diverse topics as language, the meaning of work, the different ways women and men plan ahead, and how attitudes would change if men menstruated. She has also continued the political analysis and reporting she began in her days with *New York* magazine, although in recent years she has concentrated on the way in which political events affect women's lives.

Steinem has said that, if she were to name a high point in all her years as a writer, "It might be the two sleepless days I spent as an invited outside scribe for diverse caucuses at the 1977 National Women's Conference." The conference was a public, government-sponsored event at which women from all over America met in Houston to vote on the legal and governmental changes they believed were needed to remove barriers to equality. These recommendations were then passed on to Congress and to the president. As a member of the conference's planning commission, Steinem had helped ensure that the delegates represented every age, racial, and economic group in the country. The conference also included women who opposed the ERA and other feminist goals. Nevertheless, it passed many pro-equality resolutions and was an inspiring gathering for the 2,000 voting delegates and some 15,000 women who came to help and learn.

Steinem was deeply moved by the sight of so many women, from every conceivable background, gathered together to agree on common goals. She was particularly happy to work with the minority group delegations—from Vietnamese refugees to representatives of Indian tribes—until they agreed on a resolution about the needs of all women of color in the United States. When the full conference passed the resolution, Steinem felt a surge of pride at being a writer. Helping these women find language that enabled them to agree with one another—language that also helped convince nonminority women to adopt the resolution—was at least as fulfilling as seeing her articles in print.

Steinem saw Houston as a landmark in the history of the women's movement and a personal landmark as well: "the sort of milestone that divides our sense of time. Figuring out the date of

In an article about novelist Alice Walker, pictured here, Steinem charged that the white male literary establishment had denied writers such as Walker the recognition they deserved.

any other event now means remembering: was that before or after Houston?" As a planner for the conference, Steinem had worried so much about its success that, when the time came, she found herself wanting to stay home "or just indefinitely delay this event about which I cared too much." After the conference, she realized that she had been prey to irrational fears. In her nearly 10 years as a feminist, she had learned that individual women could be strong and loyal to each other, but she still had not believed that women *as a group* could be. Houston showed Steinem that women could "conduct large, complex events that celebrated our own diversity."

The decade since Houston held many other milestones for Steinem. In 1980 her mother died. Long after her last breath, both of Ruth Steinem's daughters sat in her hospital room as she had requested—one of Mrs. Stein-

em's many fears was that a coma might be mistaken for death, and she would be buried alive. Since those troubled years in Toledo, Mrs. Steinem had spent some time in competently run, humane institutions, and her mental health had improved somewhat. She managed to live on her own for a while, then in an apartment in her older daughter's house. Every year, she and Steinem took vacations together. Mrs. Steinem regained some of her zest for

Delegates to the 1977 National Women's Conference, including Bella Abzug (in hat) and Betty Friedan (right), parade through the streets of Houston. The four-day event was a high point in Steinem's career as a feminist activist.

life, read widely, and made friends easily.

But Ruth Steinem still had spells of terrible fear, when she could not bear to go outdoors or to stay home alone. She worried constantly about money even though there was no longer any need, and she would still plunge into depression when reminded of her past. After Ruth's death, her younger daughter wrote: "I miss her, but perhaps no more in death than I did in life. Dying seems less sad than having lived too little."

A year after her mother's death, Steinem returned to Smith College for the Class of 1956's 25th reunion. Like most events in her recent life, the Smith reunion was food for feminist thought. Steinem noticed, for instance, that the women most likely to attend the reunion had achieved the goals that went along with the "Smith image" of the 1950s: suburban housewives and mothers who had married successful men. Steinem had worried that the fact that she was unmarried and childless—and a public figure— might isolate her from former college friends. But she found that being back in the dorms made everyone act as if the past 25 years had never happened.

She did find some resentment at her slender figure. "Being famous is not the worst crime a woman can commit," she discovered. "The worst crime is to be thin." Steinem tried to explain that

Steinem strolls through the Oberlin College campus with her mother in the early 1970s. Ruth Steinem, who died in 1980, had been forced to leave Oberlin years earlier because of financial problems.

she was a "food junkie" herself and had always struggled to maintain her weight. Even so, she found she "could not always connect across the weight barrier." The only classmate who later published a hostile comment about Steinem said nothing about what Steinem had said or done at the reunion, only that she was "an anach-

Steinem and Ms. staff member Pat Carbine examine a Ms. cover story about women's attitudes toward food. Steinem is a self-confessed "food junkie."

ronism from the 1970s in size-six designer jeans talking sisterhood."

Despite this minor unpleasantness, Steinem had a great time at her reunion. She was delighted with Smith's new president, a woman and a feminist. And, true to form, Steinem helped make the reunion into a consciousness-raising event by making political placards to be carried in the college's Alumnae Day Procession. The procession was an old tradition in which each graduating class marched across campus in order of seniority. It was common for the marchers, who always wore white and held roses, to carry signs—but not signs with slogans like Steinem's: THE SECOND WAVE OF FEMINISM SALUTES THE FIRST. WE SURVIVED JOE MCCARTHY—WE CAN SURVIVE REAGAN AND THE MORAL MAJORITY. '56 REMEMBERS OUR SISTERS WHO DIED OF ILLEGAL ABORTIONS—DON'T LET IT HAPPEN AGAIN. WOMEN GET MORE RADICAL WITH AGE.

When march officials saw these signs, they made Steinem and her placard-carrying classmates march at the end of the procession. But the Class of

'66 invited the sign-carriers to join them, and soon some bystanders began applauding and shouting "Good for you, give 'em hell!" The new black graduates clapped loudest of all and raised their fists in solidarity. Although Steinem's group had felt uneasy about using the procession to make political statements, now many of them and their younger friends had happy tears in their eyes.

That same year, Steinem went back to Toledo for reunions of a less formal variety. She met women from her old working-class neighborhood whom she had not seen since her youth. Few had been able to attend college at all, much less a privileged four-year school such as Smith; most had started working outside the home at an early age to support themselves and their families.

Steinem was struck by how "alive, outrageous, full of energy and self-confidence" these women were. Years before many middle-class women would discover feminism, some of these Toledo women had sued local factories for job discrimination. Others were attending college for the first time, where they would encourage their younger, wealthier classmates to fight for social justice. Comparing her experiences in Toledo to her years at Smith, Steinem began to believe that Toledo, not Smith, had given her the background she needed to become an independent woman. "How odd," Steinem wrote, "to find, after all these years, that I might owe my own survival to the very East Toledo neighborhood I worked so hard to escape."

The following year, 1982, brought a milestone for *Ms.*: the 10th anniversary of the magazine's first full edition. Dozens of other feminist publications had come and gone in the past 10 years, but *Ms.* had endured. Circulation kept growing, letters kept pouring in. The most common theme of these letters had not changed since *Ms.* first hit the newsstands: Women were still writing in, "Thank you, now I know I'm not alone."

Ms. had helped dozens of new writers get started and brought greater recognition to many experienced but neglected women writers. Its articles on the arts, politics, and society influenced opinions all over America. And in its first 10 years, the *Ms.* organization had also expanded to include much more than a magazine. It had sponsored collections of feminist writings, a children's book and record, a vast national educational network, along with countless other literary, artistic, and political projects.

Partly because of its success, the magazine has been (and continues to be) the target of right-wing pressure. Over the years *Ms.* has been subject to many attacks—from bomb threats to censorship campaigns aimed at keep-

ing the magazine out of school libraries. None of the physical threats were
carried out, but censorship drives
against *Ms.* have increased in recent
years.

Ms. marked its 10th birthday with
celebrations across the nation and a
special Anniversary Issue. Steinem introduced the Anniversary Issue with
an article in which she reflected on the
past and future of the women's movement. She began by describing the
ways in which women's lives have
changed:

> *Now*, we are becoming the men we
> wanted to marry. Ten years ago, we
> were trained to marry a doctor, not be
> one. *Now*, kids are beginning to have
> two parents—and other adult friends.
> Ten years ago, Dr. Spock and psychiatry
> were still insisting only Mothers
> Mattered. *Now*, networks of women-
> helping-women are a force in every
> town, profession, racial and economic
> group. Ten years ago, mostly white
> groups of women were still
> consciousness-raising in the privacy of
> the living room.

Steinem went on to say that the success of the women's movement meant
that its opponents were now taking
feminism seriously enough to fight
back. But feminists were getting better
every year at knowing their adversary's
tactics. After describing some of these
methods, Steinem went on to give "a
random sample of some ways women
are proceeding anyway." In the 1980s

and thereafter, she wrote, women
would and should

—Reintroduce the ERA, and keep fighting for its ratification.

—Get rid of the ideal of the "super-
woman," who is expected to have a
full-time job outside the home while
handling all the housework and child
rearing.

—Stop domestic violence. "Statistically
speaking," Steinem pointed out, "the
most dangerous place for an American
woman is not the street. It's her own
home."

—Encourage women to use their voting power to support feminist causes
and candidates.

"No worthwhile battle," she concluded, "can be won only once. Now
we have a past to celebrate—and a big
future to plan. It's the end of the Beginning. The stage is set."

The year after *Ms.*'s 10th anniversary,
Steinem published *Outrageous Acts
and Everyday Rebellions*. It was a milestone in her life as a writer: her first
full-length book in 20 years and, she
said, her first real book, because she
considers her India guidebook and her
beach anthology only "semibooks."
Outrageous Acts includes Steinem's favorite articles from the previous 20
years—among them her Bunny story,
parts of her campaign diaries, and 5
profiles of women—as well as new essays about her life and that of her
mother.

Steinem is searched by a Washington, D.C., policewoman following her 1984 arrest during a protest against South African racial segregation.

Steinem turned 50 in 1984. As with her 40th birthday, she made this personal milestone an occasion for public celebration and feminist reflection. Her birthday party—which, as a practical feminist, she combined with a *Ms.* Foundation fund-raiser—was a $250-a-plate bash at New York's Waldorf-Astoria Hotel. Some 750 politicians, writers, actors, and activists joined Steinem's close family and friends to eat, drink, dance, and pay tribute to Steinem. Actor Alan Alda, a longtime feminist, told the crowd that Steinem had changed his life. "She brought the world together," said former congresswoman Bella Abzug. TV host Phil Donahue, the emcee of the evening, said that Steinem had "made sisterhood a household word."

Several guests at the celebration exemplified the way in which women's roles had changed since Steinem's conversion to feminism. Sally Ride, the astronaut, was there, as were newscasters Jane Pauley and Diane Sawyer and many businesswomen and politicians whose jobs had rarely, if ever, been held by women 20 years earlier.

Of all the toasts and speeches that evening, perhaps the most touching tribute came from Rosa Parks, then 71. Mrs. Parks, a black woman whose refusal to sit in the back of a Montgomery, Alabama, bus in 1955 sparked the massive civil rights protests of the 1960s, was heartfelt in praising Steinem

Outrageous Acts was a critical success; even *Playboy* magazine's reviewer praised the new, autobiographical essays. The book was also a best-seller. For the first time, Steinem was able to put away some money, and she started a savings plan for her old age.

Sally Ride, the first American woman in space, arrives in Cape Canaveral, Florida, for her historic 1983 flight. The astronaut was among the many celebrities who turned out for Steinem's 50th birthday celebration.

Steinem's birthday party was widely reported in the celebrity columns; *People* magazine called her a "feminist fatale." Steinem at 50 did seem more playful and openly fun-loving than she had 10 years earlier. She posed for photographs in New York's Central Park, flourishing a yellow balloon, grinning and throwing her arms wide for the camera. That same year, she even let a woman photographer from *People* magazine snap a photo of her relaxing in a bubble bath in her hotel room after a book tour. (Although it was quite modest, Steinem had second thoughts about this photo, and she asked *People* not to print it—but when they refused, she laughed and took it in stride.) The year she turned 50 she did an impromptu tap dance during a TV interview. Clearly, Steinem was having a good time with her new, less-serious image—but she was also proving a point: that women can now reach 50 and still "remain whole and sexual people in the public eye."

Steinem made this remark in a 1984 *Ms.* article titled "Fifty Is What Forty Used to Be—and Other Thoughts on Growing Up." Women were living longer than ever before, she wrote, and older women had more chances to feel like attractive and productive human beings.

for "fighting for the rights of all people . . . regardless of sex, creed, or color."

Dressed in a long, ice-blue gown, with a rhinestone snake bracelet on her upper arm, Steinem informed the guests, "Now you know what I'm going to be doing for the next half-century. I'm going to be living up to tonight." She then urged the guests to "have a hell of a good time."

The only real worry that aging has caused Steinem so far is a "sudden and heightened sense of how very, very much I still have to do before I die.'' Steinem's life since her 50th birthday has probably been more active than ever before. She has continued to travel, lecture, and raise funds for *Ms.* and for various equal-rights projects. Although running for political office is one of the few activities she has always refused to consider, she still works long hours as a strategist for both male and female feminist candidates. In 1986 she also appeared as a regular correspondent for the "Today Show,"

and worked to help put together a syndicated feminist television program.

That same year Steinem completed *Marilyn: Norma Jeane*, a full-length book about the star Marilyn Monroe, illustrated with photographs by George Barris. In *Marilyn: Norma Jeane*, Steinem describes the real woman behind the media's sex-kitten image. The real Monroe, as Steinem portrays her, was intelligent, generous, and often very lonely, a committed actress with deeply held beliefs who hated being

Steinem congratulates two of Ms. *magazine's 1985 "Women of the Year," Democratic politician Geraldine Ferraro (center), the first woman nominated by a major party for the vice-presidency, and rock star Cyndi Lauper (right).*

Gloria Steinem continues to champion feminist causes. Of the women's movement she says, "We are in it for life — and for our lives."

joked about and treated as a dumb blond. Steinem asked whether feminism might have given Monroe self-esteem and strength and perhaps prevented her 1962 suicide. Steinem felt akin to the actress because, like Steinem, Monroe had fought to escape from a hard childhood. Steinem also saw her younger self in Monroe's intellectual and emotional insecurity, and in the way she had difficulty convincing other people to take her seriously as an adult with brains and opinions. For much of 1986 and early 1987, Steinem traveled across the United States and to England to promote her new book, which has been a great success with the public and most critics.

It is hard to sum up Steinem's varied career, especially because, by her own reckoning, she has another four or five decades of work ahead of her. And it is impossible to guess what Steinem's epitaph might be when her life and work are done. But many years ago, when Steinem was a new but already much-celebrated feminist, an interviewer half-jokingly asked her what statement she herself would like to have inscribed on her tombstone.

The interviewer reports that after a pause, Steinem responded "in that unforgettable Ohio timbre that is either enthralling or irritating thousands these days: 'Oh, I guess, HERE LIES A GOOD PERSON. I mean that in the Jewish sense, a person with a good heart. That's how I'd like to be remembered, as somebody who tried to change things, to leave a little less pain in this world.' "

FURTHER READING

Friedan, Betty. *The Feminine Mystique.* New York: Dell, 1984.

———. *It Changed My Life: Writings on the Women's Movement.* New York: Random House, 1976.

Gornick, Vivian, and Barbara K. Moran, eds. *Women in Sexist Society: Studies in Power and Powerlessness.* New York: Basic Books, 1971.

Morgan, Robin, ed. *Sisterhood is Powerful: An Anthology of Writings from the Women's Liberation Movement.* New York: Random House, 1970.

O'Neill, William L. *Everyone Was Brave: The Rise and Fall of Feminism in America.* New York: Quadrangle, 1969.

Steinem, Gloria. "After Black Power, Women's Liberation." *New York,* April 7, 1969.

———. *The Beach Book.* New York: Viking, 1963.

———. *Marilyn: Norma Jeane.* New York: H. Holt & Co., 1986.

———. "The Moral Disarmament of Betty Coed." *Esquire,* September 1962.

———. *Outrageous Acts and Everyday Rebellions.* New York: Holt, Rinehart, and Winston, 1983.

CHRONOLOGY

March 25, 1934	Gloria Steinem is born in Toledo, Ohio
c. 1944	Steinem's father, Leo, leaves home
1944–51	Steinem cares for her emotionally disturbed mother and attends school irregularly
1951	Moves to Washington, D.C., to live with her sister and complete her high school education
1952	Enrolls in Smith College Begins writing political articles
1956	Graduates magna cum laude from Smith College Accepts a two-year fellowship to study in India
1957	Writes *The Thousand Indias*, a guidebook for the Indian government
1960	Moves to New York City; embarks on a journalism career
1962	Publishes her first major article, "The Moral Disarmament of Betty Coed"
1963	Publishes "A Bunny's Tale" and *The Beach Book*
1968	Cofounds *New York* magazine Attends feminist meeting while on assignment for *New York*
1969	Writes her first feminist article, "After Black Power, Women's Liberation"
1969–74	Lectures on feminism throughout the United States
1970	Wins Penney-Missouri Journalism Award for "After Black Power, Women's Liberation"
1971	Helps found *Ms.* magazine, the National Women's Political Caucus, and the Women's Action Alliance
1977	Plans and attends the National Women's Conference in Houston, Texas
1983	Publishes *Outrageous Acts and Everyday Rebellions*, a collection of essays and articles
1984	Celebrates her 50th birthday at a gala fund-raiser for the *Ms.* Foundation
1986	Publishes *Marilyn: Norma Jeane*, a biography of Marilyn Monroe

INDEX

abortion, 41, 67, 68, 71, 79, 80

Abzug, Bella, 80, 84, 101

"After Black Power, Women's Liberation" (Steinem), 70

Alda, Alan, 101

Animal Farm (Orwell), 39

antifeminists, 89, 95

antiwar movement, 70

Baldwin, James, 59

Barris, George, 103

Beach Book, The (Steinem), 57

Bellow, Saul, 59

Benton, Bob, 49

Blixen, Karen, 14

"Bunny's Tale, A" (Steinem), 51, 55, 57, 68, 71, 100

Capote, Truman, 59

caste system, 42, 43

censorship, 99, 100

Central Intelligence Agency (CIA), 87

Chávez, César, 14, 61, 64

Chisholm, Shirley, 80, 84, 86

civil rights movement, 62, 70, 101

Clark Lake, 24, 26, 32

cold war, 39

Color Purple, The (Walker), 94

consciousness-raising, 70, 76

Crime and Punishment (Dostoyevski), 39, 45

Darkness at Noon (Koestler), 39

Davis, Angela, 61

Democratic convention (1972), 84–86

Democratic party, 39, 64, 65

Democratic presidential primary (1972), 80

Desmond, Paul, 60

Dinesen, Isak *see* Blixen, Karen

Donahue, Phil, 101

East Toledo, 28, 32

Edgar, Joanne, 17

Equal Rights Amendment (ERA), 89, 95, 100

Esquire, 13, 49, 51

Felker, Clay, 17, 61, 62

Feminine Mystique, The (Friedan), 69

feminism, 13, 14, 17, 19, 21, 41, 67–75, 77, 80, 88–90, 95, 100, 101

Ferraro, Geraldine, 86

"Fifty Is What Forty Used To Be—And Other Thoughts on Growing Up" (Steinem), 102

Finkelstein, Nina, 17

Frederick, Pauline, 59

Friedan, Betty, 69, 80, 84, 86, 87, 89

Galbraith, John Kenneth, 57, 64, 82

Gandhi, Mahatma, 42

Geneva, 39

Glamour, 59

Gone With the Wind (Mitchell), 32

Graham, Katharine, 17

Great Depression, the, 24, 26

Guinzberg, Tom, 60

Hefner, Hugh, 51, 54, 55

Help!, 48, 49

Ho Chi Minh, 45

Houston, 94–96

Howard, Pamela, 18

Hughes, Dorothy Pitman, 75, 77

Humphrey, Hubert, 64

Independent Research Service, 47

India, 39, 40, 42, 43, 45, 47, 57

Johnson, Lyndon, 64

Johnson, Rafer, 75

Kennedy, Florynce, 75

Kennedy, John F., 47, 58, 93

Kennedy, Robert, 14, 64

King, Dr. Martin Luther, Jr., 62, 64

Koestler, Arthur, 39

lesbianism, 87
Little Women (Alcott), 32
Lovelace, Linda, 93
Marilyn: Norma Jeane (Steinem), 103, 105
McCall's, 86
McCarthy, Eugene, 64
McGovern, George, 64, 81–86
Millett, Kate, 80
Monroe, Marilyn, 103, 105
"Moral Disarmament of Betty Coed, The" (Steinem), 51
Moreau, Jeanne, 14
Ms., 14, 15, 17–21, 61, 73, 77, 79, 80, 84, 86, 88–91, 93, 99–102
National Organization for Women (NOW), 69, 71, 79
National Student Organization, 47, 87
National Women's Conference, 94
National Women's Political Caucus (NWPC), 84, 85
Nessim, Barbara, 48
New Delhi, 43
Newsweek, 13, 86
New York, 14, 17, 18, 19, 62, 64, 67, 70, 71, 94
New York City, 14, 20, 40, 47, 48, 57, 77, 80
New York Times Magazine, 59, 61
Nichols, Mike, 60
1984 (Orwell), 39
Nixon, Pat, 93
Nixon, Richard, 64, 85, 93
Onassis, Jacqueline Kennedy, 93
Orwell, George, 39
Outrageous Acts and Everyday Rebellions (Steinem), 34, 75, 101
Parker, Dorothy, 59
Parks, Rosa, 101
Pauley, Jane, 101
Peacock, Mary, 17
People, 102
Playboy, 51, 54, 55, 101

Playboy Club, 51–55
Pogrebin, Letty Cottin, 17
Pottinger, Stanley, 90
presidential campaign (1972), 85
Redstockings, 67, 68, 70, 71, 87
Republican convention (1972), 85
Ribicoff, Abraham, 81, 83, 84
Ride, Sally, 101
Rockettes, 32, 35
"Ruth's Song (Because She Could Not Sing It)" (Steinem), 29
Sargent, Herb, 60
Sawyer, Diane, 101
Seventeen, 61
Show, 51
"Sisterhood" (Steinem), 20, 21
Sloan, Margaret, 75
Smith College, 37–40, 42, 97–99
Smith, Liz, 49
Steinem, Gloria
    and abortion, 41
    adolescence, 27–30, 32, 35
    birth, 24
    childhood, 24, 25
    cofounds *Ms.*, 14, 15, 17, 73
    early journalism career, 48, 49
    education, 25, 29, 35, 37, 38–40
    engagement, 40
    feminist leader, 13, 70, 71, 88–91, 93
    fiftieth birthday, 101
    free-lance writer, 45, 49, 57, 58, 59
    in India, 39, 42, 43, 49
    lecturer, 73, 75, 76, 77
    as "Marie Ochs," 51, 52, 54
    and national politics, 61, 62, 64, 65, 82–85, 87
    at Smith College twenty-fifth reunion, 98, 99
Steinem, Joseph (grandfather), 23
Steinem, Leo (father), 25, 27, 30, 58
Steinem, Pauline (grandmother), 23
Steinem, Ruth Nuneviller (mother), 23–28, 30, 32, 35, 37, 90, 96, 97

INDEX

Steinem, Susanne (sister), 24, 26, 35, 37,90
Stevenson, Adlai, 82
Supreme Court, 79, 80
Tale of Two Cities, A (Dickens), 28
"That Was the Week That Was," 59
Thousand Indias, The (Steinem), 45
Time, 13, 71, 72, 77
"Today Show," 103
Toledo, 35, 37, 38, 40, 45, 49, 96, 99
Vietnam War, 65, 70
Viking Press, 57, 60

Walker, Alice, 93
Washington, D.C., 35, 37, 84
Weaver, Lloyd, 64
"What It Would Be Like If Women Win"
    (Steinem), 71, 72
Women's Action Alliance, 84
women's liberation movement *see*
    feminism
Women's Strike for Equality, 80
women's suffrage movement, 23
World War II, 26, 27

PICTURE CREDITS

AP/Wide World Photos: pp. 12, 15, 46, 56, 72, 76, 81, 87, 88, 96, 98; The Bettmann Archive: pp. 25, 30, 43; Neal Boenzi/NYT Pictures: p. 8; Capital Cities/ABC Inc.: p. 20; *Ms.* magazine: p. 91; Ann Phillips: p. 73; Reuters/Bettmann Newsphotos: pp. 52, 59; Smith College: p. 41; Gloria Steinem: pp. 21, 22, 24, 26, 27, 28, 31, 33, 34, 36, 39, 50, 97; UPI/Bettmann Newsphotos: pp. 16, 18, 19, 29, 38, 42, 44, 48, 53, 54, 55, 58, 60, 61, 62, 63, 65, 66, 68, 69, 70, 74, 78, 82, 83, 85, 86, 90, 92, 94, 95, 101, 102, 103, 104

Carolyn Daffron writes fiction, practices law, and lives with her husband and young son in Philadelphia. A graduate of the University of Chicago and Harvard Law School, she has worked for Philadelphia's Community Legal Services and currently teaches part-time at Rutgers University.

❖   ❖   ❖

Matina S. Horner is president of Radcliffe College and associate professor of psychology and social relations at Harvard University. She is best known for her studies of women's motivation, achievement, and personality development. Dr. Horner serves on several national boards and advisory councils, including those of the National Science Foundation, Time Inc., and the Women's Research and Education Institute. She earned her B. A. from Bryn Mawr College and Ph.D. from the University of Michigan, and holds honorary degrees from many colleges and universities, including Mount Holyoke, Smith, Tufts, and the University of Pennsylvania.